# THE AI MILLIONAIRE MAKER:

## Wealth Creation with Artificial Intelligence

## BY

## GABY DALLANS

# CONTENTS

# 1. Introduction

In the corridors of history, some moments redefine the trajectory of humanity, sparking revolutions that echo across generations. As we stand on the precipice of the 21st century, a new force is emerging, poised to transform not just industries but the very fabric of our existence. Welcome to the era of The AI Millionaire Maker.

In the following pages, we embark on a journey into the heart of innovation, where the convergence of human ingenuity and artificial intelligence creates a synergy that can shape destinies. The digital age has bestowed upon us tools of unprecedented potential, and at the forefront of this revolution is the enigmatic force known as Artificial Intelligence.

Picture a world where algorithms can decipher complex patterns, predict future trends, and unlock the secrets of wealth creation. This isn't a vision confined to the realms of science fiction; it is the reality we find ourselves in today. The AI Millionaire Maker is not just a book; it is a manifesto for those who dare to dream beyond conventional boundaries, for those who understand that the future belongs to those who can harness the power of AI.

As we delve into the intricacies of this transformative technology, we will explore how AI is disrupting industries, propelling businesses to unprecedented heights, and creating a new breed of millionaires. Gone are the days when wealth creation was solely within the grasp of a select few; now, the tools of financial liberation are distributed across lines of code and neural networks.

But this isn't just a guide to accumulating riches. The AI Millionaire Maker is a call to action, a blueprint for those who seek personal prosperity and wish to contribute to the evolution of our global society. The following pages will illuminate the path to financial freedom, offering insights into the strategies employed by visionaries who have harnessed AI to navigate the complexities of our ever-changing world.

Join me as we unlock the mysteries of Artificial Intelligence, demystify its applications, and chart a course toward a future where prosperity is not a privilege but a promise. The journey begins here, and the destination is a world where The AI Millionaire Maker becomes a reality for those bold enough to embrace the opportunities.

## The Rise of Artificial Intelligence

A few phenomena have shaped the trajectory of civilization as profoundly as the rise of artificial intelligence (AI). This chapter explores the multifaceted aspects of this technological revolution, tracing its roots, examining its current state, and contemplating the potential future it heralds.

The journey of artificial intelligence begins with the dreams and aspirations of visionaries. From Alan Turing's groundbreaking work on computing in the 1930s to the Dartmouth Conference in 1956, where the term "artificial intelligence" was first coined, humanity embarked on a quest to create machines capable of intelligent behavior. The initial years were marked by optimism and the belief that machines could emulate human thought processes.

Despite the initial enthusiasm, the field of AI faced numerous challenges. In the 1970s and 1980s, the AI community encountered what came to be known as "AI winters" — periods of reduced funding and interest due to unmet expectations and technological limitations. The elusive goal of creating machines with human-like intelligence seemed increasingly distant.

The turning point came with the advent of machine learning and the abundance of big data. In the late 20th century, algorithms capable of learning from data and making decisions without explicit programming gained prominence. The rise of the internet and the digitalization of vast datasets fueled this new wave of AI.

At the heart of AI's resurgence lies deep learning, a subset of machine learning inspired by the human brain's neural networks. Neural networks with multiple layers (deep neural networks) demonstrated remarkable capabilities in image and speech recognition tasks. The development of powerful GPUs accelerated the training of these complex models, enabling AI systems to surpass human performance in various domains.

As AI capabilities advanced, so did ethical concerns. The rise of autonomous systems, algorithmic bias, and the potential misuse of AI raised questions about accountability, transparency, and the societal impact of these technologies. Policymakers, ethicists, and technologists grappled with establishing ethical guidelines to ensure AI's responsible development and deployment.

The integration of AI into various industries has reshaped economies worldwide. From healthcare and finance to manufacturing and transportation, AI has optimized processes, improved decision-making, and created new opportunities. Simultaneously, concerns about job displacement and the need to reskill the workforce have become central themes in the discourse surrounding AI's economic impact.

The pursuit of artificial general intelligence (AGI), where machines possess the ability to perform any intellectual task that a human being can, remains the ultimate goal. However, this quest poses unprecedented challenges. Researchers grapple with understanding consciousness, common-sense reasoning, and the ethical implications of creating entities with human-like cognitive capabilities.

The rise of AI prompts reflection on the evolving relationship between humans and machines. As AI systems become more integrated into daily life, questions arise about the societal implications of widespread automation, the nature of human-AI collaboration, and the role of AI in addressing global challenges such as climate change and healthcare.

The trajectory of AI points toward a future where the boundaries between the artificial and the natural blur. Quantum computing, neuro-inspired architectures, and advances in robotics are poised to usher in new frontiers. The possibilities and potential risks of these developments underscore the need for ongoing dialogue, international collaboration, and a commitment to ethical AI research.

The rise of artificial intelligence is an unfolding saga that encapsulates the triumphs and tribulations of human ingenuity. As society grapples with the transformative power of AI, the imperative lies not only in advancing technological capabilities but also in fostering a collective responsibility to ensure that these advancements serve the betterment of humanity. The narrative of AI continues to be written, and the choices made today will shape the course of tomorrow.

## The Promise of Wealth Creation

The integration of artificial intelligence has emerged as a transformative force, propelling individuals toward unprecedented financial success. This chapter explores "The AI Millionaire Maker" phenomenon and its profound impact on shaping the promise of wealth creation in the 21st century.

Artificial intelligence, with its ability to analyze vast amounts of data, identify patterns, and make informed predictions, has become a game-changer in various industries. From finance to healthcare, AI has proven its prowess in optimizing processes, reducing costs, and enhancing decision-making. The convergence of AI and wealth creation has given birth to what is now known as "The AI Millionaire Maker."

At the heart of The AI Millionaire Maker lies the unprecedented access to and utilization of data. AI algorithms thrive on data, and the more comprehensive and diverse the dataset, the more accurate and valuable the predictions. Wealth creation through AI involves harnessing this power, leveraging data-driven insights to identify lucrative investment opportunities, predict market trends, and optimize financial strategies.

One of the most prominent applications of AI in wealth creation is within the realm of algorithmic trading and investment. The AI Millionaire Maker relies on sophisticated algorithms that analyze market conditions, assess risk factors, and execute trades at speeds and accuracies beyond human capabilities. This automated approach to trading has proven to be a key driver in generating substantial returns for those who embrace this technology.

AI extends its influence into personal finance, providing individuals with tailored wealth management solutions. The AI Millionaire Maker doesn't just focus on large-scale investment; it caters to the individual, offering personalized financial advice, budgeting strategies, and investment portfolios based on unique circumstances and goals. This democratization of financial planning empowers individuals to navigate the complex landscape of wealth creation confidently.

While The AI Millionaire Maker holds immense promise, it has challenges. The reliance on algorithms introduces risks of algorithmic bias, data breaches, and ethical concerns. Striking a balance between maximizing financial gains and ensuring responsible AI practices is crucial for the sustainable development of wealth creation through AI.

As AI continues to evolve, so does The AI Millionaire Maker. The future promises even more sophisticated algorithms, improved predictive analytics, and a broader integration of AI into diverse financial sectors. The individuals who position themselves at the forefront of this technological wave are poised to accumulate wealth and contribute to shaping the economic landscape for generations to come.

"The AI Millionaire Maker" represents a paradigm shift in the way we approach and achieve wealth creation. By harnessing the power of artificial intelligence, individuals have the opportunity to navigate the complexities of financial markets with unprecedented precision and efficiency. As we continue to explore the potential of AI in wealth creation, it is essential to remain vigilant, addressing ethical considerations and ensuring that the benefits of this technological revolution are accessible to a broad spectrum of society. The future belongs to those who embrace the transformative potential of The AI Millionaire Maker and chart a course toward a prosperous and sustainable financial future.

## 2. Understanding Artificial Intelligence

Artificial Intelligence (AI) has emerged as a transformative force reshaping how we live, work, and interact with the world. This chapter aims to provide a comprehensive overview of AI, exploring its history, key concepts, applications, and the ethical considerations surrounding its development and deployment.

The roots of AI can be traced back to ancient times when myths and legends depicted artificial beings with human-like intelligence. However, the formal development of AI as a field of study began in the mid-20th century. The term "Artificial Intelligence" was coined by John McCarthy in 1955, who organized the Dartmouth Conference and considered the birth of AI as an academic discipline.

AI refers to the capability of a machine to imitate intelligent human behavior. This includes learning from experience, adapting to new situations, understanding natural language, and solving problems. AI is not a single technology but a combination of various approaches and techniques.

AI is often categorized into two main types: Narrow AI (or Weak AI) and General AI (or Strong AI). Narrow AI is designed to perform a specific task or a set of functions, such as image recognition or language translation. In contrast, General AI could understand, learn, and apply knowledge across a wide range of tasks, similar to human intelligence.

A crucial subset of AI is machine learning (ML), which involves algorithms that enable machines to learn from data and improve their performance over time without explicit programming. Supervised, unsupervised, and reinforcement learning are common paradigms within machine learning.

Deep learning is a specialized machine learning form involving neural networks with multiple layers (deep neural networks). This approach has shown remarkable success in tasks such as image and speech recognition, natural language processing, and playing strategic games like chess and Go.

The applications of AI are vast and continue to expand across various industries. From healthcare and finance to manufacturing and entertainment, AI is driving innovation. Examples include virtual personal assistants, recommendation systems, autonomous vehicles, and medical diagnosis tools.

As AI technology advances, ethical concerns arise regarding issues like bias in algorithms, job displacement due to automation, privacy concerns, and the potential misuse of AI in surveillance and warfare. Striking a balance between innovation and responsible AI development is crucial.

The future of AI promises exciting developments, including advancements in natural language processing, explainable AI, and the integration of AI with other emerging technologies like the Internet of Things (IoT) and blockchain.

Understanding Artificial Intelligence is essential for navigating the complexities of our rapidly evolving technological landscape. As AI continues to shape our world, it is imperative to approach its development and deployment with a thoughtful and ethical mindset to harness its potential for the benefit of humanity.

## What is AI?

Artificial Intelligence, often abbreviated as AI, is a transformative field that has captivated the imagination of scientists, researchers, and the general public alike. As technology advances at an unprecedented pace, AI plays an increasingly prominent role in shaping how we live, work, and interact with the world. This chapter aims to unravel the intricacies of AI, exploring its origins, defining characteristics, and the diverse applications that make it a revolutionary force in the modern era.

The roots of AI can be traced back to ancient times, with philosophical inquiries into the nature of human thought and intelligence. However, the formal inception of AI as a field of study can be pinpointed to the mid-20th century. In 1956, John McCarthy coined the term "artificial intelligence" during the Dartmouth Conference, which is often considered the birthplace of AI as a discipline. McCarthy, along with other pioneers like Marvin Minsky, Claude Shannon, and Allen Newell, laid the foundation for the development of intelligent machines.

At its core, AI refers to creating systems that can perform tasks that typically require human intelligence. These tasks encompass a wide range of activities, from problem-solving and decision-making to language understanding, perception, and even creative endeavors. AI systems are designed to mimic or replicate cognitive functions, allowing machines to analyze information, learn from it, and make informed decisions.

AI can be categorized into two main types: Narrow AI (or Weak AI) and General AI (or Strong AI). Narrow AI is designed to perform specific tasks and excel within a limited domain. Examples include virtual personal assistants like Siri and Alexa and recommendation algorithms used by streaming services. In contrast, General AI is a form of artificial intelligence that can understand, learn, and apply knowledge across a broad spectrum of tasks, akin to human intelligence. As of now, General AI remains largely theoretical and has yet to be fully realized.

A significant subset of AI is machine learning, a methodology that empowers systems to learn from data and improve their performance over time. Deep learning has gained prominence within machine learning. Inspired by the structure and function of the human brain, deep learning involves neural networks with multiple layers (hence the term "deep"). These networks can automatically learn hierarchical representations of data, allowing them to tackle complex tasks such as image and speech recognition.

The applications of AI are vast and diverse, spanning numerous industries and domains. In healthcare, AI is used for diagnostic purposes, drug discovery, and personalized treatment plans. In finance, AI aids in fraud detection, algorithmic trading, and risk management. The automotive industry leverages AI for autonomous vehicles, while customer service benefits from chatbots and virtual assistants.

As AI continues to evolve, ethical considerations become increasingly important. Questions surrounding job displacement, bias in algorithms, and the responsible use of AI technologies prompt ongoing discussions. Striking a balance between innovation and ethical considerations is crucial to harnessing the full potential of AI while minimizing potential risks and negative consequences.

Artificial Intelligence is a testament to humanity's quest to create intelligent machines to augment our capabilities and improve our lives. From its humble beginnings in the mid-20th century to the present day, AI has evolved into a powerful force shaping the future of technology and society. Understanding the fundamentals of AI is essential as we navigate the complexities and opportunities that this transformative field presents.

Artificial Intelligence (AI) is a broad and rapidly evolving field encompassing various approaches and methodologies. The classification of AI is often based on its capabilities, functions, and the level of human-like intelligence it exhibits. This chapter will explore the main types of AI and their characteristics.

Narrow AI, or Weak AI, refers to systems designed and trained for a specific task. These AI systems excel in performing a well-defined set of operations but lack the broad cognitive abilities associated with human intelligence. Examples include speech recognition, image recognition, and natural language processing applications. Narrow AI is prevalent daily, powering virtual assistants like Siri and recommendation algorithms on streaming platforms.

General AI, or Strong AI, represents the concept of machines possessing the ability to understand, learn, and apply knowledge across diverse tasks at a level comparable to human intelligence. Unlike Narrow AI, which is specialized in one domain, General AI would be capable of performing any intellectual task that a human being can. Achieving General AI remains an aspirational goal in the field, as it involves replicating the complexity and adaptability of the human mind.

Artificial Narrow Intelligence (ANI) is a subtype of Narrow AI that refers explicitly to systems designed for a singular task but can outperform humans in that area. ANI excels in chess-playing programs, language translation, and image recognition. Despite its limitations to a specific domain, ANI can exhibit remarkable precision and efficiency, often surpassing human capabilities in those particular tasks.

Artificial General Intelligence (AGI) is the AI that can understand, learn, and apply knowledge in any domain, mirroring the broad cognitive abilities of human beings. AGI is a theoretical concept that, if realized, would signify a machine's capacity to perform intellectual tasks at a human level across a wide range of activities. Researchers and scientists are actively exploring ways to develop AGI, but it remains an elusive goal.

Superintelligent AI refers to a hypothetical future AI system that surpasses human intelligence and the most brilliant minds on

Earth. This level of intelligence could potentially lead to unforeseen consequences, making it a topic of ethical and existential concern. Researchers and experts debate the likelihood and implications of achieving superintelligent AI, as it poses challenges and risks that demand careful consideration.

Machine Learning (ML) is a subset of AI that focuses on developing algorithms and models that enable machines to learn from data and improve their performance over time. Neural Networks, inspired by the human brain's structure, are crucial to many ML applications. Deep Learning, a subfield of ML, involves neural networks with multiple layers, allowing for more complex representations and higher accuracy in tasks like image and speech recognition.

Reactive Machines are AI systems that operate based on predefined rules and programmed responses, lacking the ability to learn or adapt from experience. Limited Memory AI, conversely, incorporates past experiences into decision-making processes, enabling more adaptive behavior. These distinctions play a crucial role in shaping the capabilities and limitations of AI systems in various applications.

The landscape of AI is diverse, ranging from specialized systems designed for specific tasks to ambitious endeavors aiming for human-like intelligence. As technology advances and research progresses, the lines between these types of AI may blur, and new paradigms emerge, ushering in a future where artificial intelligence becomes an integral part of our daily lives in ways we can only begin to imagine.

Understanding the critical components of AI systems is essential for enthusiasts and professionals. This chapter explores the fundamental building blocks that make AI systems capable of mimicking human intelligence, processing vast amounts of data, and making informed decisions. By dissecting the core components, we gain insight into the intricate mechanisms that power the realm of AI.

At the heart of any AI system lies data – the raw material from which intelligence is crafted. AI systems lack the foundation to learn and adapt without a robust and diverse dataset. Quality data, sourced and curated meticulously, forms the lifeblood that nourishes machine learning algorithms. Whether it's images, text, audio, or video, the richness and variety of data determine the system's ability to comprehend and respond to the world.

The engine that propels AI forward is the set of algorithms collectively known as machine learning. These algorithms empower AI systems to detect patterns, make predictions, and learn from experience. Supervised learning, unsupervised learning, and reinforcement learning are prominent paradigms that guide how AI interprets and processes information. The continuous refinement of these algorithms is crucial to enhancing the accuracy and efficiency of AI systems.

A subset of machine learning, deep learning, is a powerful technique inspired by the human brain's neural networks. Neural networks, composed of layers of interconnected nodes (neurons), enable AI systems to model complex relationships within data. The depth and complexity of these networks allow for hierarchical feature extraction, making them adept at tasks such as image and speech recognition. The advancement of deep learning has significantly contributed to the breakthroughs in AI in recent years.

For AI systems to comprehend and interact with humans, they must master the intricacies of language. Natural Language Processing (NLP) equips AI with the ability to understand, interpret, and generate human language. From chatbots that engage in conversations to language translation systems, NLP is indispensable in bridging the communication gap between humans and machines.

The ability of AI systems to perceive and interpret visual information is made possible by computer vision. Through image and video analysis, computer vision enables machines to recognize objects, faces, and even emotions. This component is integral in applications ranging from autonomous vehicles to facial recognition systems, underscoring its importance in AI.

The ultimate goal of many AI systems is to make informed decisions. Reinforcement learning, a subset of machine learning, focuses on training models to make sequential decisions by learning from feedback. Whether it's a game-playing AI mastering complex strategies or a robotic system navigating its environment, reinforcement learning is pivotal in enabling AI to act autonomously.

Addressing ethical considerations and mitigating biases is crucial as AI systems become more prevalent. Understanding the societal impact of AI, ensuring fairness in algorithms, and implementing transparency are essential components to foster responsible AI development and deployment.

The key components of AI systems encompass diverse technologies and methodologies. From the foundation of quality data to the sophisticated algorithms that enable learning and decision-making, each component plays a vital role in shaping the capabilities of AI. As the field continues to evolve, a holistic understanding of these components will be essential for navigating the complexities of AI in the future.

Artificial Intelligence (AI) has rapidly evolved from a theoretical concept to a transformative force that permeates various aspects of our daily lives. As we delve into the applications of AI, it becomes evident that its impact is vast and multifaceted, revolutionizing industries and reshaping the way we interact with technology.

AI is making significant strides in healthcare, enhancing diagnostics, treatment, and patient care. Machine learning algorithms analyze medical images, aiding in the early detection of diseases such as cancer. Natural language processing (NLP) enables computers to understand and respond to human language, facilitating improved communication between patients and healthcare providers through virtual assistants. AI is also instrumental in drug discovery, accelerating the identification of potential candidates and reducing the time and cost of bringing new medications to market.

AI has become a cornerstone in the financial sector, revolutionizing how transactions are conducted, risks are assessed, and fraud is detected. Algorithmic trading, powered by AI, processes vast amounts of financial data in real time, making split-second decisions to optimize trading strategies. Machine learning models analyze patterns to detect anomalies and prevent fraudulent activities, ensuring the security of financial transactions. Additionally, AI-powered chatbots and virtual assistants enhance customer service in the financial industry, providing instant responses to inquiries and streamlining processes.

In education, AI is reshaping traditional teaching methods and personalizing learning experiences. Intelligent tutoring systems adapt to individual student needs, providing customized lessons and feedback. AI-driven educational platforms analyze student performance data to identify strengths and weaknesses, allowing educators to tailor instruction plans. Natural language processing facilitates the development of chatbots and virtual tutors, providing students instant support and guidance. Furthermore, AI plays a crucial role in automating administrative tasks, freeing up educators to focus on teaching.

The automotive industry is undergoing a transformative shift with the integration of AI into autonomous vehicles. Machine learning algorithms process data from sensors, cameras, and radar systems to navigate and make real-time decisions on the road. AI enhances safety by predicting and preventing accidents, optimizing traffic flow, and reducing human error. Autonomous vehicles have the potential to revolutionize transportation, making it more efficient, sustainable, and accessible.

AI is reshaping the retail landscape, enhancing customer experiences, and optimizing business operations. Recommendation systems analyze customer preferences and behaviors, providing personalized product suggestions. Computer vision technologies enable cashier-less stores, where AI-powered cameras track items and automatically charge customers as they exit. AI-driven supply chain management improves inventory forecasting, reducing waste and ensuring products are readily available. AI-powered virtual shopping assistants enhance customer service, providing instant support and information.

As the digital landscape expands, so does the need for robust cybersecurity measures. AI plays a pivotal role in identifying and mitigating cyber threats. Machine learning models analyze patterns in network traffic to detect anomalies indicative of cyber attacks. AI-driven threat intelligence systems continuously adapt to evolving threats, providing real-time protection against malicious activities. Autonomous response systems leverage AI to automatically respond to and neutralize cyber threats, reducing response time and minimizing potential damage.

In entertainment, AI is transforming content creation, curation, and consumption. Recommendation algorithms analyze user preferences to suggest movies, music, and other content tailored to individual tastes. AI-driven content creation tools assist in generating music, art, and even writing, pushing the boundaries of creativity. Virtual characters and AI-powered storytelling enhance gaming experiences, providing more immersive and dynamic narratives.

AI is playing a crucial role in addressing environmental challenges. Machine learning models analyze ecological data to monitor and predict natural disasters, enabling timely responses and mitigating the impact on communities. AI-driven optimization algorithms contribute to energy efficiency, reducing waste and carbon emissions. Powered by AI, precision agriculture enhances crop yield by analyzing weather patterns, soil conditions, and crop health data.

AI is streamlining recruitment processes, talent management, and employee engagement in human resources. AI-driven tools analyze resumes and candidate profiles to identify the best fit for job positions. Chatbots assist in answering employee queries and providing information on company policies. Predictive analytics powered by AI help in workforce planning and talent retention strategies.

Beyond specific industries, AI is significantly impacting addressing societal challenges. Predictive analytics and machine learning models assist in identifying patterns of poverty, helping governments and organizations develop targeted interventions. AI is also employed in disaster response, analyzing data to coordinate rescue efforts and provide aid to affected areas.

The applications of Artificial Intelligence are vast and continue to expand, offering unprecedented opportunities to transform industries and improve various aspects of our lives. As AI technologies mature, their integration into diverse domains promises to create more efficient, intelligent, and adaptive systems, ushering in an era of innovation and progress. However, ethical considerations and responsible deployment are paramount to ensuring that AI benefits humanity and aligns with our shared values.

Artificial Intelligence (AI) has evolved from a theoretical concept to a powerful force that permeates various aspects of our daily lives. Its applications are diverse and span numerous industries, bringing about transformative changes in how we live, work, and interact. In this chapter, we will explore some of the most prominent applications of AI, shedding light on how it is revolutionizing different sectors.

One of the most promising and impactful applications of AI is in healthcare. AI technologies are leveraged to enhance diagnostic accuracy, streamline treatment plans, and improve patient outcomes. Machine learning algorithms can analyze vast amounts of medical data, from patient records to imaging scans, to identify patterns and make predictions. This aids healthcare professionals in early disease detection, personalized treatment recommendations, and drug discovery.

IBM Watson, a cognitive computing system, is being used to assist oncologists in identifying personalized, evidence-based treatment options for cancer patients. By analyzing a vast array of medical literature, clinical trial data, and patient records, Watson provides valuable insights to guide healthcare decisions.

AI is reshaping the landscape in the financial industry by automating processes, detecting fraud, and optimizing investment strategies. Machine learning algorithms analyze market trends, predict stock prices, and execute trades at speeds impossible for human traders. AI-powered chatbots provide customer support and facilitate seamless transactions, while fraud detection systems use pattern recognition to identify and prevent unauthorized activities.

High-frequency trading relies heavily on AI algorithms to make split-second decisions based on market data. These algorithms can analyze vast datasets and execute trades at speeds that human traders cannot match, improving efficiency and responsiveness in financial markets.

AI is making significant inroads in education, offering personalized learning experiences and automating administrative tasks. Intelligent tutoring systems use machine learning to adapt to individual student needs, providing targeted feedback and resources. AI-driven platforms analyze student performance data to identify areas for improvement, allowing educators to tailor their teaching methods accordingly.

The language learning platform Duolingo employs AI algorithms to personalize lessons for users. As individuals progress through language modules, the system adapts based on their strengths and weaknesses, ensuring a customized learning experience that enhances overall proficiency.

AI optimizes production processes, improves quality control, and enhances overall efficiency in manufacturing. Robotic systems equipped with AI can perform complex tasks with precision, reducing errors and increasing productivity. Predictive maintenance, powered by machine learning, helps prevent equipment failures by forecasting when machinery will likely require attention.

Tesla's manufacturing plants utilize AI for automation and quality control. Robots with computer vision and machine learning algorithms assemble and inspect vehicles, ensuring high-quality standards and efficient production.

AI is transforming the entertainment industry by personalizing content recommendations, creating immersive experiences, and automating content production. Streaming services use recommendation algorithms to suggest movies and shows based on user preferences, while AI-powered tools assist in video and music production, from editing to composition.

Netflix employs a sophisticated recommendation system that analyzes user behavior, viewing history, and preferences to suggest content tailored to individual tastes. This enhances user satisfaction and engagement on the platform.

In transportation, AI drives innovations in autonomous vehicles, traffic management, and logistics. Self-driving cars use AI algorithms, including computer vision and sensor fusion, to navigate and make real-time decisions on the road. AI is also crucial in optimizing traffic flow, reducing congestion, and improving overall transportation efficiency.

Waymo, a subsidiary of Alphabet Inc. (Google's parent company), utilizes AI technologies to power its fleet of autonomous vehicles. These vehicles can navigate complex urban environments, interpret traffic signals, and respond to dynamic road conditions.

The applications of AI are multifaceted and continue to expand as technology advances. From healthcare and finance to education and entertainment, AI is reshaping industries, enhancing efficiency, and unlocking new possibilities. As AI continues to evolve, its impact on society will likely be profound, ushering in unprecedented innovation and transformation. Understanding these applications is crucial for navigating the evolving landscape of artificial intelligence and harnessing its potential for the betterment of humanity.

We explored the foundational concepts and principles that define Artificial Intelligence (AI). Now, let's delve into the myriad applications of AI across various domains, showcasing its transformative potential in shaping our present and future.

AI has made significant strides in revolutionizing healthcare, offering innovative solutions to longstanding challenges. Machine learning algorithms analyze medical data to diagnose diseases, predict patient outcomes, and personalize treatment plans. Additionally, AI facilitates the discovery of new drugs and enhances the efficiency of clinical trials, paving the way for more effective and targeted medical interventions.

In the financial sector, AI is a powerful tool for risk management, fraud detection, and investment strategy optimization. Predictive analytics and machine learning models analyze vast datasets to identify patterns, mitigate risks, and inform investment decisions. Chatbots powered by natural language processing (NLP) assist in customer service, providing real-time support and enhancing user experience.

AI has the potential to transform education by personalizing learning experiences. Intelligent tutoring systems adapt to individual student needs, providing targeted feedback and customizing educational content. Furthermore, AI aids in automating administrative tasks, allowing educators to focus more on teaching and fostering student engagement.

AI-driven automation has increased efficiency, reduced costs, and improved product quality in manufacturing. Robotics, powered by AI algorithms, perform complex tasks precisely, while predictive maintenance models help minimize downtime by anticipating equipment failures. Smart factories leverage AI to optimize production processes and enhance supply chain management.

The development of autonomous vehicles represents a groundbreaking application of AI in transportation. Machine learning algorithms process vast amounts of sensor data to enable vehicles to navigate, perceive their surroundings, and make real-time decisions. This technology can revolutionize the automotive industry, making transportation safer and more efficient.

AI has transformed retail by enhancing customer experiences and optimizing business operations. Recommendation engines use machine learning to analyze customer preferences and suggest personalized product recommendations. AI-powered chatbots provide instant customer support, and computer vision enables cashier-less checkout systems, streamlining the shopping process.

The ever-evolving landscape of cybersecurity relies heavily on AI for threat detection and prevention. Machine learning algorithms analyze network traffic patterns, identify anomalies, and detect potential security breaches in real time. AI-driven tools enhance the speed and accuracy of threat response, fortifying digital ecosystems against cyberattacks.

AI plays a crucial role in environmental monitoring and conservation efforts. Remote sensing technologies, powered by machine learning, analyze satellite imagery to track deforestation, monitor wildlife habitats, and assess the impact of climate change. AI models contribute valuable insights for sustainable resource management and biodiversity preservation.

In the entertainment industry, AI is employed for content recommendation, personalized streaming services, and content creation. Algorithms analyze user preferences to suggest movies, music, and other forms of entertainment. AI-generated content, including art and music, showcases the creative potential of machine learning.

AI has the potential to address societal challenges and contribute to social good. Applications range from predicting and preventing disease outbreaks to optimizing resource allocation during humanitarian crises. AI-powered tools can assist in disaster response, poverty alleviation, and education accessibility, demonstrating the positive impact of technology on global issues.

The applications of AI are vast and diverse, touching almost every aspect of our lives. As technology advances, AI's potential to drive positive change and innovation across various industries is boundless. The ethical considerations and responsible deployment of AI will be crucial in harnessing its benefits while mitigating potential risks.

It becomes imperative to scrutinize the challenges and limitations that accompany this revolutionary technology. While AI has made significant strides, it has its challenges. In this chapter, we will explore AI's multifaceted challenges and limitations, shedding light on the intricacies that shape its development and application.

One of the foremost challenges in AI is its inherent dependence on data. Machine learning algorithms learn patterns and make predictions based on the data they are trained on. If the data is biased or incomplete, it can lead to skewed results and reinforce existing inequalities. Addressing bias in AI algorithms is an ongoing challenge, as it requires a nuanced understanding of the sources of bias and a commitment to creating fair and representative datasets.

The ethical considerations surrounding AI are becoming increasingly complex. As AI systems become more autonomous, questions arise about their decision-making processes. Issues such as accountability, transparency, and the potential for AI to be used unethically pose significant challenges. Striking a balance between innovation and ethical responsibility is crucial for the responsible development and deployment of AI technologies.

"artificial intelligence" encompasses many technologies and approaches, leading to a lack of shared understanding. AI is often portrayed in popular media and culture in ways that may not align with its capabilities. This misrepresentation can create unrealistic expectations and hinder informed public discourse. Educating the public about the capabilities and limitations of AI is essential for fostering a more accurate understanding of this powerful technology.

The technical challenges in AI development are numerous and diverse. Issues such as overfitting, underfitting, and the curse of dimensionality can affect the performance of machine learning models. Creating AI systems that can adapt to dynamic and unpredictable environments remains a significant hurdle. Advancements in addressing these technical challenges are crucial for the continued progress of AI.

The increased integration of AI into critical systems raises concerns about the security of these technologies. Malicious actors could exploit vulnerabilities in AI systems to manipulate outcomes or compromise sensitive information. Developing robust security measures and protocols is essential to safeguard against potential threats to AI applications.

AI models, intense learning models, often require substantial computational resources for training and inference. This resource intensiveness poses challenges regarding energy consumption, environmental impact, and accessibility. Finding ways to optimize and make AI more resource-efficient is a pressing concern for the sustainable development of this technology.

Acknowledging and addressing its challenges and limitations is paramount. From data biases to ethical dilemmas and technical hurdles, the journey to harness the full potential of AI is fraught with obstacles. However, by fostering interdisciplinary collaboration, promoting ethical guidelines, and investing in research and development, we can mitigate these challenges and shape a future where AI contributes positively to society. In the following chapters, we will explore potential solutions and future trajectories for artificial intelligence.

## Evolution of AI Technologies

From its early theoretical foundations to today's sophisticated systems, AI has undergone a remarkable transformation, impacting various aspects of human life and reshaping industries. This chapter explores the key phases and milestones in the evolution of AI technologies.

The inception of AI can be traced back to the 1950s when pioneers like Alan Turing and John McCarthy laid the theoretical groundwork. Turing's seminal work on computability and the Turing Test set the stage for envisioning machines that could simulate human intelligence. McCarthy and others organized the Dartmouth Conference in 1956, marking the birth of AI as a field of study.

The next phase witnessed the development of Symbolic AI, focusing on rule-based systems and logic. Researchers explored the creation of expert systems that could emulate human expertise in specific domains. Despite early successes, these systems faced limitations in handling uncertainty and real-world complexity.

The late 1980s and 1990s saw a period known as the "AI winter," characterized by waning interest and reduced funding due to unmet expectations. However, during this time, the field experienced a shift towards machine learning. The advent of algorithms like backpropagation for training neural networks and the emergence of support vector machines laid the foundation for a new era.

Advances in computational power and the availability of vast amounts of data spurred the renaissance of AI. Machine learning algorithms and intense learning gained prominence. Breakthroughs like the ImageNet competition demonstrated the potential of deep neural networks in image recognition, triggering a wave of interest and investment.

The integration of AI into daily life became more pronounced in the 2010s. Natural Language Processing (NLP) advanced, enabling machines to understand and generate human language. Chatbots, virtual assistants, and language translation tools have become commonplace. Robotics also saw significant developments, with AI-powered robots entering industries, healthcare, and households.

As AI applications became more widespread, concerns about ethical implications and bias gained prominence. The field of Responsible AI emerged, emphasizing transparency, fairness, and accountability in AI development. Efforts to address algorithm biases and establish ethical guidelines became essential for AI research and implementation.

Looking ahead, the future of AI holds exciting possibilities. Explainable AI aims to enhance the interpretability of AI systems, making their decision-making processes more transparent. Quantum computing, with its potential to handle complex AI tasks exponentially faster, presents a new frontier for exploration.

The evolution of AI technologies is a testament to human ingenuity and the relentless pursuit of understanding and replicating intelligence. From theoretical concepts to real-world applications, AI has come a long way, impacting diverse fields and shaping how we live and work. As we navigate the future, AI's ethical considerations and responsible development will be crucial in ensuring that these technologies contribute positively to society.

# Key Concepts and Terminology

Establishing a common language is essential for effective communication and understanding. This chapter aims to elucidate key concepts and terminology that will serve as the foundation for exploring subsequent chapters.

To embark on this intellectual journey, it is imperative to establish a shared understanding of fundamental terms. Concepts such as knowledge, information, data, and wisdom will be defined to provide a solid framework for the following chapters.
Data: Raw, unprocessed facts and figures.

**Information:** Processed and organized data that conveys meaning.

**Knowledge:** Information that is understood and applied.

**Wisdom:** The ability to make sound judgments based on knowledge and experience.

Understanding the progression from data to wisdom involves navigating the information spectrum. This spectrum encompasses the stages of data, information, knowledge, and wisdom, illustrating the evolution of information as it gains context and significance.

Many fields contribute to the collective understanding of the world. A shared vocabulary facilitates interdisciplinary collaboration. This section explores how terminology from various disciplines interconnects and enriches our comprehension.

**Cross-disciplinary Terminology:** Common terms that bridge gaps between disciplines.

Interdisciplinary Challenges: The nuances of communication across diverse fields.

Different disciplines often operate within specific paradigms and frameworks. Unpacking these concepts is crucial for appreciating the underlying structures that shape the lens through which information is interpreted.

**Paradigms:** Fundamental beliefs and assumptions that guide a discipline.

**Frameworks:** Organizational structures that provide a conceptual scaffold.

In an age dominated by technology, specific terms have gained prominence. Familiarity with these concepts is essential for navigating the digital landscape.

**Big Data:** Massive datasets that require advanced processing. Artificial Intelligence: Machines mimicking human cognitive functions.

**Blockchain**: Decentralized and secure digital ledger technology. As our reliance on digital systems grows, understanding cybersecurity terms becomes paramount. Encryption: The process of encoding information for secure transmission.

**Malware**: Malicious software designed to harm or exploit systems.

**Firewall:** A barrier that prevents unauthorized access to a network. Navigating the ethical terrain of information and technology is critical to any discussion. Key terms related to ethics will be explored.

**Privacy:** The right to control personal information.

**Transparency:** Openness and clarity in actions and decisions.

**Bias:** Prejudice or favoritism in data or algorithms.

In a more interconnected world than ever, understanding terms related to globalization and cultural dynamics is imperative.

**Cultural Relativism:** Judging a culture by its standards.

**Global Citizenship**: A sense of belonging to a broader global community.

**Cultural Appropriation:** Adoption of elements from one culture by members of another.

To prepare for the future, exploring emerging concepts and terminology is essential.

**Internet of Things (IoT):** Interconnected devices communicating and sharing data.

**Augmented Reality (AR)**: Overlapping digital content with the real world.

**Quantum Computing:** Leveraging quantum mechanics for advanced computation.

In a world characterized by rapid change, adapting and understanding evolving terminology is crucial.

**Agile:** A flexible and iterative approach to project management.

**Disruptive Innovation:** Innovations that fundamentally alter existing markets.

As we delve into subsequent chapters, these key concepts and terminology will serve as the intellectual compass guiding our journey through the intricacies of knowledge and discovery.

## 3. The Foundations of AI Wealth

Artificial Intelligence (AI) has emerged as a transformative force, reshaping industries and economies. The notion of AI wealth goes beyond mere financial gain; it encompasses the creation of value, innovation, and the sustainable development of societies. This chapter delves into the foundational pillars that underpin AI wealth and explores the multifaceted dimensions of its impact.

At the heart of AI lies an insatiable appetite for data. Data is not just a commodity; it is the raw material that fuels AI algorithms, enabling them to learn, adapt, and make informed decisions. The more diverse and high-quality the data, the more robust and effective the AI system becomes. The foundations of AI wealth are deeply rooted in the ethical and responsible collection, management, and utilization of data.

AI algorithms are the brainpower driving the wealth-generating capabilities of AI. Whether it's machine learning, deep learning, or other AI techniques, the efficiency and accuracy of algorithms determine the success of AI applications. The continuous refinement and development of algorithms and a commitment to transparency and fairness form the second pillar of AI wealth.

The synergy between humans and machines is a crucial aspect of AI wealth. Rather than viewing AI as a threat to human employment, the focus should be on how AI can augment human capabilities. The collaborative efforts of humans and AI can lead to unprecedented productivity, innovation, and problem-solving, contributing to economic growth and prosperity.

Sustainable AI wealth is contingent upon ethical considerations and responsible AI practices. Ensuring fairness, transparency, and accountability in AI systems is imperative to prevent unintended consequences and biases. Developing and adhering to ethical guidelines contribute to the long-term trust and acceptance of AI technologies, fostering a conducive environment for their continued growth.

Building and maintaining AI wealth requires a skilled workforce capable of navigating the complexities of AI technologies. Investing in education and skill development programs is essential to empower individuals with the knowledge and expertise needed to harness the full potential of AI. This pillar not only supports economic growth but also ensures inclusivity in benefiting from AI-driven advancements.

A robust regulatory framework is essential for fostering AI innovation and safeguarding against potential risks. Governments and regulatory bodies play a pivotal role in creating a conducive environment for AI wealth by establishing guidelines that promote responsible AI development, protect user privacy, and mitigate potential ethical concerns.

Geographical boundaries do not confine AI wealth. Global collaboration and cooperation among nations, organizations, and researchers are essential for maximizing the benefits of AI on a worldwide scale. Information sharing, joint research initiatives, and open dialogue facilitate the responsible development and deployment of AI technologies for the collective good.

The foundations of AI wealth are multifaceted, intertwining technological prowess with ethical considerations, human ingenuity, and collaborative efforts. Navigating this dynamic landscape requires a holistic approach that recognizes the interconnectedness of these pillars. By building on these foundations, societies can harness the transformative power of AI to create lasting value, foster innovation, and propel themselves into a future enriched by the possibilities of artificial intelligence.

## Data: The Fuel of AI

In the vast landscape of artificial intelligence (AI), there exists a singular element that serves as the lifeblood, the catalyst, and the driving force behind its evolution: data. Data has emerged as the most valuable resource in the digital era, propelling AI into unprecedented realms of innovation and capability. This chapter explores the intricate relationship between AI and data, shedding light on the pivotal role that data plays as the fuel that powers the engine of artificial intelligence.

At the heart of every intelligent system lies the insatiable appetite for data. In its various forms, AI thrives on information – the raw material from which it learns, adapts, and evolves. The genesis of AI's reliance on data can be traced back to its roots in machine learning. Unlike traditional rule-based systems, machine learning algorithms are designed to extract patterns and insights from data, continuously refining their understanding through exposure to new information.

While the quantity of data available is undoubtedly crucial, the quality of the data holds equal, if not more significant, significance.

The saying "garbage in, garbage out" controls the realm of AI. Flawed or biased data can lead to distorted outcomes, reinforcing prejudices and misconceptions. Therefore, the meticulous curation and preprocessing of data become paramount to the success of AI applications, ensuring that the algorithms are fed with reliable, unbiased, and representative information.

In the symbiotic relationship between AI and data, a virtuous cycle unfolds. As AI algorithms are exposed to diverse and expansive datasets, they learn, adapt, and enhance their performance. This continuous loop of learning and improvement allows AI systems to stay relevant in dynamic environments. The more data they ingest, the more refined their predictions and decisions become, creating a self-reinforcing loop that propels the technology forward.

As AI increasingly permeates various facets of society, ethical considerations surrounding data usage emerge. Questions of privacy, consent, and the responsible handling of sensitive information become critical. Striking a balance between leveraging data for innovation and safeguarding individual rights and liberties poses a constant challenge. Ethical frameworks and regulations are emerging to guide the ethical use of data in AI applications, aiming to ensure that the power of data is wielded responsibly.

While data is undeniably the fuel that propels AI, challenges and limitations persist. Data bias, privacy concerns, and the sheer volume of data to be processed pose formidable obstacles. Addressing these challenges requires a multidisciplinary approach involving data scientists, engineers, ethicists, policymakers, and society.

Looking ahead, the future of AI is inexorably linked to the evolution of data ecosystems. The concept of federated learning, where models are trained across decentralized devices without exchanging raw data, is gaining prominence to preserve privacy while harnessing the collective intelligence of interconnected devices. Additionally, advancements in data generation, such as synthetic data and simulations, are poised to reshape the landscape, providing AI systems with diverse and comprehensive datasets.

In conclusion, data stands as the indispensable fuel of AI, driving its progress, shaping its capabilities, and influencing its impact on society. As we navigate the intricate interplay between data and artificial intelligence, we must tread carefully, mindful of the ethical implications and societal ramifications. Both challenges and boundless potential characterize the journey ahead as we continue to unlock the transformative power of data in AI.

## Machine Learning: Building Intelligent Systems

Machine Learning (ML) has emerged as a pivotal force, propelling us into an era where intelligent systems are integral to our daily lives. This chapter delves into the intricate process of building intelligent systems through the lens of Machine Learning, exploring the fundamental concepts, methodologies, and the transformative impact on various domains.

At its core, machine learning is a subfield of artificial intelligence (AI) that focuses on developing algorithms and models that enable computers to learn from data. Unlike traditional rule-based programming, where explicit instructions are provided, ML empowers systems to understand patterns and make informed decisions autonomously.

Machine Learning encompasses various learning paradigms, each suited for specific scenarios. Supervised learning involves training a model on labeled data, where the algorithm learns to map input features to corresponding output labels. On the other hand, unsupervised learning deals with unlabeled data, seeking patterns and relationships within the information. Reinforcement learning introduces the concept of agents learning from interactions with an environment, receiving feedback as rewards or penalties.

Building intelligent systems with Machine Learning involves several vital components. The data pipeline is critical, encompassing data collection, preprocessing, and feature engineering. Robust datasets, representative of real-world scenarios, are the foundation for successful models. Feature engineering involves selecting and transforming relevant features to enhance the model's ability to discern patterns.

Choosing a suitable ML model is a crucial step in the process. Decision trees, neural networks, support vector machines, and ensemble methods are among the myriad options available. The model is trained on a portion of the data, and its performance is evaluated on a separate validation set. This iterative process involves fine-tuning model hyperparameters to achieve optimal results.

The development of intelligent systems brings forth ethical considerations that demand scrutiny. Bias in training data, interpretability of models, and the potential societal impact are among the ethical challenges that developers must address. Striking a balance between technological advancement and responsible AI implementation is imperative for fostering trust and ensuring ethical AI practices.

Machine Learning has permeated diverse fields, revolutionizing industries and augmenting human capabilities. In healthcare, predictive models aid in disease diagnosis and treatment planning. In finance, ML algorithms analyze market trends and manage risk. Autonomous vehicles leverage ML for navigation and decision-making, while natural language processing powers virtual assistants and language translation.

Despite the remarkable progress, building intelligent systems with Machine Learning is challenging. Ongoing concerns are overfitting, lack of interpretability, and the need for massive labeled datasets. Future directions include:

- Advancements in explainable AI.
- Addressing ethical considerations.
- The integration of ML with other cutting-edge technologies, such as quantum computing.

Building intelligent systems with Machine Learning is an exciting expedition into the realms of possibility. As we navigate the intricacies of algorithms, data, and ethical considerations, the evolving landscape of ML redefines the boundaries of what machines can achieve. With a steadfast commitment to responsible development, the potential for positive transformation across industries is boundless. As we forge ahead, the collaborative efforts of researchers, developers, and policymakers will play a pivotal role in shaping the future of intelligent systems powered by Machine Learning.

### Deep Learning: Unraveling Complex Patterns

The field of deep learning has emerged as a powerful tool for unraveling complex patterns in data. As we delve deeper into neural network architectures and advanced algorithms, we find ourselves equipped to tackle intricate problems that were once deemed impossible. This chapter explores the essence of deep learning in deciphering complex patterns and sheds light on the underlying principles that make it a transformative force in artificial intelligence.

Complex patterns are pervasive in our world, from the intricate structures of biological organisms to the convoluted relationships in financial markets. Traditional machine learning techniques often need to catch up when faced with these intricate patterns, struggling to capture the nuances and interdependencies inherent in complex datasets. This limitation has paved the way for deep learning, a paradigm miming the human brain's ability to understand and learn intricate patterns.

At the heart of deep learning are neural networks, computational models inspired by the architecture of the human brain. These networks consist of interconnected layers of artificial neurons, each layer learning hierarchical representations of the input data. The depth of these networks—the number of layers—distinguishes deep learning from shallow machine learning models, enabling them to learn complex features and relationships.

One key aspect of unraveling complex patterns is the use of unsupervised learning. Unlike supervised learning, where the algorithm is trained on labeled data, unsupervised learning allows the model to identify hidden structures and patterns within unlabeled data. Techniques such as autoencoders and generative adversarial networks (GANs) excel in discovering intricate features that might go unnoticed by traditional methods.

Deep learning's prowess in unraveling complex patterns is further enhanced by transfer learning. In this paradigm, models trained on one task can be repurposed for another, leveraging the knowledge gained from a related domain. This approach is beneficial when labeled data is scarce, as the pre-trained models bring a wealth of learning features that can be fine-tuned for the problem.

While deep learning has proven to be a game-changer in pattern recognition, it has challenges. The need for vast amounts of labeled data, the computational resources required for training deep networks, and the interpretability of complex models are all areas of ongoing research and development. Striking a balance between model complexity and generalization remains a central challenge in applying deep learning to real-world problems.

This chapter would only be complete by delving into real-world applications of deep learning in unraveling complex patterns. From healthcare diagnostics to natural language processing and image recognition, we explore success stories where deep learning has made significant strides in understanding and interpreting intricate data.

We look toward the future as we conclude this exploration into deep learning and its role in unraveling complex patterns. The field is dynamic, with continual advancements in neural network architectures, optimization algorithms, and the application of deep learning across diverse domains. The journey to unraveling the most intricate patterns in our world is ongoing, and deep learning stands as a beacon of innovation on this quest.

We will dive deeper into specific applications, methodologies, and emerging trends in the ever-evolving landscape of deep learning. As we unravel complex patterns, the potential for transformative impact across industries becomes increasingly apparent, heralding a new era in artificial intelligence.

## 4. AI in Business: A Profitable Partnership

Staying ahead of the competition requires more than just traditional strategies. The integration of Artificial Intelligence (AI) has emerged as a transformative force, reshaping industries and redefining the way businesses operate. This chapter explores the symbiotic relationship between AI and business, shedding light on how this partnership yields profitability and innovation.

Artificial Intelligence, with its ability to process vast amounts of data and make intelligent decisions, has become a cornerstone of strategic business initiatives. Whether automating routine tasks, optimizing processes, or uncovering actionable insights from data, AI has proven to be a game-changer for businesses across sectors.

One of the key advantages of integrating AI into business operations is the significant boost in efficiency. AI-powered systems can automate repetitive and time-consuming tasks, allowing human resources to focus on more complex and value-added activities. From streamlining supply chain logistics to automating customer support, businesses are witnessing operational transformations that translate into cost savings and improved productivity.

In the customer-centric age, providing a personalized and seamless experience is paramount. AI algorithms analyze customer behavior, preferences, and interactions to tailor products and services. AI-powered chatbots and virtual assistants offer real-time support, enhancing customer satisfaction. Businesses leveraging AI in this way retain existing customers and attract new ones through positive word-of-mouth and enhanced brand reputation.

Informed decision-making is the bedrock of successful business strategies. AI processes vast datasets at unprecedented speeds, extracting valuable insights that human analysis may overlook. Predictive analytics, powered by AI, empowers businesses to foresee market trends, optimize inventory levels, and make strategic decisions with a higher probability of success. The result is a competitive edge in an ever-changing business landscape.

AI catalyzes innovation, revolutionizing how products are conceived, developed, and brought to market. Machine learning algorithms analyze market trends, consumer preferences, and competitor strategies, aiding in the ideation phase. In fields like healthcare and finance, AI is accelerating research and development, leading to breakthroughs that were once thought impossible.

As businesses become increasingly digital, the need for robust cybersecurity measures is more critical than ever. AI algorithms can detect anomalies in network behavior, identify potential threats, and respond in real-time. This proactive approach safeguards sensitive data and instills confidence in customers and partners, fostering trust in an era where data breaches are a prevalent concern.

While the benefits of AI in business are undeniable, ethical considerations and responsible AI practices cannot be overlooked. Striking the right balance between innovation and ethical considerations is crucial for long-term success. Moreover, collaboration between businesses, academia, and regulatory bodies is essential to create frameworks that ensure AI technologies' responsible deployment and usage.

AI in business is not just a buzzword; it's a strategic imperative for those aiming to thrive in the digital era. From operational efficiency to customer experience enhancement, the symbiotic partnership between AI and business is rewriting the rules of success. As enterprises navigate this transformative journey, embracing the potential of AI is not just profitable—it's a pathway to sustainable growth, innovation, and a competitive edge in the dynamic landscape of the 21st century.

# Transforming Industries with AI

Artificial Intelligence (AI) has emerged as a transformative force, reshaping industries across the globe. Integrating AI technologies into various sectors is not just a technological evolution but a revolution that has profound implications for businesses, economies, and society. In this chapter, we will explore how AI catalyzes unprecedented changes, unlocks new opportunities, and challenges traditional paradigms across diverse industries.

AI has ushered in a new era of intelligent automation, enabling industries to streamline processes, enhance efficiency, and reduce operational costs. Automation powered by AI algorithms and machine learning models has become a cornerstone in the manufacturing, logistics, and finance industries. Intelligent robots equipped with AI capabilities take over routine and labor-intensive tasks, allowing human workers to focus on more complex and creative aspects of their roles.

AI is revolutionizing diagnostics, treatment plans, and patient care in the healthcare sector. Machine learning algorithms analyze vast amounts of medical data, providing clinicians with valuable insights for accurate diagnosis and personalized treatment options. Additionally, AI-powered robotic surgery systems improve surgical precision, reduce recovery times, and enhance overall patient outcomes.

AI is playing a pivotal role in modernizing agriculture through precision farming techniques. Autonomous drones with AI algorithms monitor crop health, identify pests, and optimize irrigation. Machine learning models analyze weather patterns and historical data to predict crop yields, helping farmers make informed decisions and maximize productivity. AI-driven agricultural advancements are crucial for addressing global food security challenges.

In the financial industry, AI is transforming traditional banking and investment practices. Robo-advisors use AI algorithms to analyze market trends and provide personalized investment advice. Fraud detection systems leverage machine learning to identify and prevent suspicious activities. Blockchain technology and AI are reshaping the landscape of financial transactions, enhancing security, transparency, and efficiency.

AI is reshaping the retail landscape by enabling personalized customer experiences. Recommendation algorithms analyze customer preferences and behaviors to provide tailored product suggestions. Virtual shopping assistants powered by natural language processing enhance customer interactions, improving satisfaction and increasing loyalty. AI-driven supply chain optimization ensures efficient inventory management and timely restocking.

The transportation industry is undergoing a significant transformation with the integration of AI. Autonomous vehicles, powered by machine learning algorithms, are set to revolutionize how people and goods are transported. AI-driven traffic management systems enhance the efficiency of urban mobility, reducing congestion and improving overall transportation infrastructure. Smart cities leverage AI to optimize energy consumption, waste management, and public services.

While the transformative impact of AI on industries is evident, it also raises ethical considerations and challenges. Data privacy, bias in algorithms, and job displacement require careful consideration. Striking a balance between innovation and ethical considerations is crucial to ensuring the responsible and sustainable integration of AI technologies across industries.

The transformative power of AI is reshaping industries, driving innovation, and creating new possibilities. As businesses continue to adopt and adapt to AI technologies, it is essential to navigate the ethical challenges and ensure that the benefits of AI are equitably distributed. The journey towards a future powered by AI is dynamic, and industries must embrace collaboration, continuous learning, and ethical practices to realize this technological revolution's potential fully.

In the 21st century, the healthcare industry has undergone a transformative journey, leveraging cutting-edge technologies to enhance patient care, diagnosis, and treatment. One of the most revolutionary forces driving this transformation is Artificial Intelligence (AI). This chapter will explore how AI is reshaping the healthcare landscape, revolutionizing patient care, and contributing to the broader paradigm shift of Transforming Industries with AI.

AI has emerged as a game-changer in medical diagnostics, significantly improving the accuracy and speed of disease identification. Advanced machine learning algorithms, trained on vast datasets of medical images, can now detect anomalies in radiological scans, such as X-rays, MRIs, and CT scans, with precision that surpasses human capabilities. This expedites the diagnosis process and reduces the likelihood of human errors.

For instance, AI algorithms in radiology can identify early signs of diseases like cancer, enabling healthcare professionals to intervene at an earlier stage when treatment outcomes are generally more favorable. The ability of AI to analyze complex medical images swiftly has led to more efficient healthcare workflows, allowing clinicians to focus on developing personalized treatment plans for patients.

AI is at the forefront of enabling personalized medicine, tailoring treatment plans to individual patients based on their unique genetic makeup, lifestyle, and medical history. By analyzing vast datasets of gene information, AI algorithms can identify specific genetic markers associated with diseases and predict individual responses to various treatments.

This approach enhances treatment efficacy and minimizes adverse effects, as medications and therapies can be precisely tailored to a patient's genetic profile. The shift towards personalized medicine has transformed the healthcare industry from a one-size-fits-all model to a more targeted and practical approach, improving patient outcomes and satisfaction.

Integrating AI into healthcare systems has empowered professionals with predictive analytics capabilities, enabling them to anticipate potential health issues before they manifest. AI can identify patterns and risk factors associated with various diseases by analyzing patient data, including electronic health records, lifestyle factors, and environmental influences.

Healthcare providers can use this information to implement proactive measures, such as preventive screenings, lifestyle interventions, and targeted health education programs. The shift towards preventative care not only improves patient well-being but also helps in reducing healthcare costs by addressing issues before they escalate into more severe conditions.

AI plays a pivotal role in enhancing patient engagement and enabling remote monitoring, especially in the era of telehealth. AI-powered virtual health assistants can provide patients with real-time information, answer queries, and offer personalized health recommendations. Additionally, wearable devices equipped with AI capabilities allow continuous monitoring of vital signs, providing valuable data to healthcare providers for remote patient management.

The combination of AI-driven virtual assistants and remote monitoring devices empowers patients to actively participate in their healthcare journey actively, fostering a sense of control and accountability. This improves patient satisfaction and contributes to better health outcomes by ensuring timely interventions and adjustments to treatment plans.

While integrating AI in healthcare brings about transformative benefits, it also presents challenges and ethical considerations. Issues related to data privacy, security, and the potential for algorithmic bias require careful attention. Additionally, ensuring that AI applications align with established ethical guidelines and do not compromise the doctor-patient relationship is crucial for the responsible adoption of these technologies.

Artificial Intelligence is revolutionizing patient care in the healthcare industry, ushering in an era of precision medicine, predictive analytics, and enhanced patient engagement. The transformative impact of AI is not only improving the efficiency of healthcare delivery but also contributing to the broader narrative of Transforming Industries with AI. As technology advances, the healthcare sector must navigate the challenges and ethical considerations to harness the full potential of AI for the benefit of patients worldwide.

The financial industry has always been at the forefront of adopting technological advancements to enhance efficiency, reduce risks, and improve decision-making processes. In recent years, the integration of Artificial Intelligence (AI) has revolutionized the financial landscape, ushering in a new era of innovation and transformation. From automating routine tasks to predicting market trends, AI reshapes how financial institutions operate and deliver services.

The journey of AI in finance can be traced back to the early applications of rule-based systems for automating basic tasks.

However, with the advent of machine learning and deep learning algorithms, AI's capabilities have grown exponentially. Today, AI systems can process vast amounts of data, recognize complex patterns, and make predictions with unprecedented accuracy.

One of the primary impacts of AI in finance is the automation of routine tasks. AI-driven systems can efficiently handle tasks such as data entry, transaction processing, and customer support, freeing up human resources to focus on more strategic and complex activities. This reduces operational costs and minimizes errors associated with manual processes.

AI plays a crucial role in enhancing risk management strategies for financial institutions. Machine learning algorithms can analyze historical data to identify patterns and trends that may indicate potential risks. Furthermore, AI is instrumental in detecting fraudulent activities by continuously monitoring transactions, recognizing anomalies, and flagging suspicious behavior in real time.

The integration of AI enables financial institutions to offer highly personalized and tailored experiences to their customers. AI algorithms can analyze customer behavior and preferences through predictive analytics to provide targeted product recommendations and personalized financial advice. Chatbots powered by natural language processing (NLP) enhance customer interactions, providing instant assistance and improving overall satisfaction.

AI algorithms are reshaping the landscape of financial markets by enabling algorithmic trading and advanced market analysis. Machine learning models can analyze historical market data, identify patterns, and execute trades at speeds impossible for human traders. This improves trading efficiency and contributes to more informed decision-making in investment strategies.

In an industry heavily regulated to ensure stability and consumer protection, AI aids financial institutions in meeting compliance requirements. AI-powered systems can analyze vast volumes of data to ensure regulation adherence, detect potential compliance issues, and generate comprehensive reports. This proactive approach reduces the risk of regulatory penalties and enhances transparency in financial operations.

As AI continues to reshape the financial landscape, it brings forth ethical considerations and challenges. Issues such as bias in algorithms, data privacy concerns, and the potential for job displacement require careful consideration and proactive measures. Striking a balance between innovation and ethical practices is paramount to ensuring the responsible deployment of AI in finance.

The journey of AI in finance is far from over. The future holds exciting possibilities, including integrating blockchain technology, quantum computing, and more advanced AI applications. Collaborations between financial institutions and fintech startups will likely drive further innovation, opening new avenues for improved services, reduced costs, and increased financial inclusion.

AI's role in redefining the financial landscape is undeniable. From automating routine tasks to providing sophisticated risk management solutions, AI has become integral to the economic ecosystem. As financial institutions continue to explore and implement AI solutions, the industry is poised for further transformation, unlocking new opportunities and creating a more dynamic and efficient economic landscape. However, it is crucial to approach this transformation with a thoughtful and ethical mindset, ensuring that the benefits of AI are realized responsibly and sustainably.

Manufacturing was dominated by manual labor, heavy machinery, and linear production processes. However, the landscape has undergone a revolutionary transformation with the advent of Manufacturing 4.0, ushering in an era of intelligent factories and AI automation. This chapter explores the profound impact of artificial intelligence (AI) on the manufacturing sector, detailing how it has catalyzed unprecedented efficiency, productivity, and innovation.

Several key stages have marked the journey from traditional manufacturing to the era of Manufacturing 4.0. The First Industrial Revolution introduced mechanization, the Second brought electricity and mass production, and the Third witnessed the rise of computers and automation. Manufacturing 4.0, often called the Fourth Industrial Revolution, builds upon these advancements by seamlessly integrating digital technologies, AI, and the Internet of Things (IoT).

At the heart of Manufacturing 4.0 lies the concept of smart factories, where interconnected systems communicate and collaborate in real time. These intelligent manufacturing environments leverage sensors, actuators, and AI algorithms to optimize every aspect of the production process. From predictive maintenance to supply chain management, smart factories transform traditional manufacturing floors into dynamic, responsive ecosystems.

AI plays a pivotal role in the metamorphosis of manufacturing. Machine learning algorithms analyze vast datasets generated by sensors and machines, enabling predictive maintenance and reducing downtime. Robots with computer vision and natural language processing capabilities collaborate seamlessly with human workers, enhancing overall efficiency. AI-driven analytics empower decision-makers with actionable insights, fostering data-driven decision-making across the production lifecycle.

Manufacturing 4.0 embraces intelligent automation, where AI-powered robots and machines perform tasks with precision and adaptability. This streamlines routine processes and allows for more complex and flexible production setups. As a result, manufacturers can respond swiftly to changing market demands, producing customized products efficiently and cost-effectively.

The integration of AI in manufacturing has had a transformative impact on various industries. From automotive to pharmaceuticals, intelligent factories are redefining production standards. Quality control is enhanced through AI-powered vision systems, ensuring defects are identified and corrected in real-time. This level of precision minimizes waste and boosts customer satisfaction, creating a ripple effect across the supply chain.

While the benefits of Manufacturing 4.0 are undeniable, adopting AI in manufacturing comes with its challenges. Data security, workforce reskilling, and ethical AI implementation concerns need to be addressed. Manufacturers must invest in robust cybersecurity measures and prioritize the development of AI literacy among their workforce to navigate this paradigm shift successfully.

Manufacturing 4.0 is an ongoing journey, and the road ahead is filled with exciting possibilities. As AI evolves, smart factories will become even more intelligent and interconnected. Collaborative robots, known as cobots, will work seamlessly alongside human counterparts, and the integration of AI-driven design and simulation tools will revolutionize product development.

Manufacturing 4.0 represents a watershed moment for industries worldwide. The convergence of AI, IoT, and automation has unleashed a wave of innovation, propelling manufacturing into a new era of efficiency, agility, and sustainability. As intelligent factories become the norm rather than the exception, the manufacturing sector stands poised for unparalleled growth and evolution in the decades.

Artificial intelligence (AI) integration has emerged as a transformative force, redefining how businesses interact with their customers. This chapter delves into the profound impact of AI on retail transformation, specifically focusing on how it enhances customer experiences and contributes to the broader narrative of transforming industries.

The digital era has ushered in a new era of consumer expectations, with customers demanding seamless, personalized, and immersive shopping experiences. Traditional retail models are constantly pressured to adapt, and AI provides the tools to meet these evolving expectations. AI-driven solutions, powered by machine learning algorithms analyze vast datasets to gain insights into consumer behavior, preferences, and trends.

One of the cornerstones of AI in retail is the ability to deliver hyper-personalized experiences at scale. As customers navigate online and offline channels, AI algorithms track their preferences and behaviors, allowing retailers to tailor recommendations, promotions, and content. Whether suggesting products based on past purchases or predicting future needs, AI transforms customer interactions into highly individualized journeys.

AI-powered chatbots and virtual assistants have redefined customer service in retail. These intelligent systems provide instant responses to queries, offer product recommendations, and guide customers through their purchase journey. Natural language processing (NLP) enables these virtual assistants to understand and respond to customer inquiries with human-like proficiency, enhancing the overall customer service experience.

AI plays a pivotal role in optimizing inventory management and supply chain processes. AI algorithms make accurate predictions about product demand by analyzing historical data, market trends, and external factors. This enables retailers to optimize stock levels, reduce excess inventory, and minimize stockouts, ultimately improving customer satisfaction through product availability.

AI-driven technologies like computer vision and RFID (Radio-Frequency Identification) transform the in-store experience. Smart shelves, cashierless checkout systems, and personalized in-store navigation enhance the convenience and efficiency of shopping. With AI ensuring consistency in their shopping journey, customers can enjoy a seamless transition between online and offline channels.

AI-powered AR technologies revolutionize how customers engage with products, particularly in industries like fashion and beauty. Virtual try-ons allow customers to visualize products in real-time, creating a more immersive and interactive shopping experience. This reduces the likelihood of returns and adds a layer of excitement to the purchasing process.

As retailers leverage AI to enhance customer experiences, ethical considerations, and data privacy become paramount. Striking the right balance between personalization and respecting customer privacy is crucial. Transparent communication about data usage and implementing robust security measures are essential to building trust in AI-driven retail environments.

The integration of AI in retail marks a paradigm shift, redefining how businesses connect with their customers. By harnessing the power of AI to deliver personalized, efficient, and innovative experiences, retailers can meet and exceed customer expectations. As we navigate the transformative landscape of retail, it is evident that AI is a driving force behind the evolution of industries, paving the way for a future where customer experiences are at the forefront of innovation.

Integrating artificial intelligence (AI) into the energy sector has emerged as a transformative force, revolutionizing how industries produce, distribute, and consume energy. This comprehensive AI-driven approach enhances energy systems' efficiency and is instrumental in reducing environmental impact. This article explores the innovative applications of AI in transforming industries for a more sustainable and resilient energy landscape.

AI plays a pivotal role in optimizing the operation of smart grids, enabling real-time monitoring, control, and management of energy distribution. Machine learning algorithms analyze vast amounts of data to predict consumption patterns, identify inefficiencies, and optimize energy flow. This results in improved reliability, reduced energy losses, and better grid integration of renewable energy sources.

Predictive maintenance powered by AI algorithms allows for the early detection of equipment failures and potential issues in energy infrastructure. This extends the lifespan of critical assets, minimizes downtime, and reduces the need for emergency repairs. Intelligent sensors and AI-driven analytics enhance asset management, ensuring that resources are utilized optimally.

AI algorithms are employed to optimize the performance of energy storage systems, such as batteries. Machine learning models predict energy demand fluctuations, enabling efficient charging and discharging cycles. This maximizes the lifespan of energy storage units and facilitates better integration of intermittent renewable energy sources into the grid.

AI-driven demand response systems enable consumers to adjust their energy consumption based on real-time pricing and demand signals. Machine learning algorithms analyze historical consumption patterns to provide personalized recommendations for energy-efficient practices. This not only helps in reducing energy bills for consumers but also contributes to overall energy conservation.

AI models leverage weather data, historical trends, and satellite imagery to forecast renewable energy generation. Accurate predictions enable better grid management and planning, ensuring a smoother integration of renewable energy sources. This, in turn, enhances the reliability of renewable energy and facilitates its increased adoption.

AI empowers the development of decentralized energy systems, allowing for the efficient management of microgrids and distributed energy resources. Localized AI controllers optimize energy production and consumption at the community level, promoting resilience and reducing dependence on centralized power plants.

AI is instrumental in identifying opportunities for carbon footprint reduction across industries. Machine learning algorithms analyze data from various sources to optimize processes, reduce energy consumption, and suggest sustainable practices. This holistic approach aids industries in achieving their sustainability goals while minimizing environmental impact.

Integrating AI in the energy sector marks a significant leap toward a sustainable future. By leveraging advanced technologies, industries can optimize their energy systems, reduce environmental impact, and contribute to a more resilient and efficient global energy landscape. As AI continues to evolve, its role in transforming industries for sustainability is poised to grow, offering unprecedented opportunities for innovation and positive environmental change.

# Case Studies of AI Success Stories

Artificial Intelligence (AI) has emerged as a transformative force across various industries, revolutionizing how businesses operate and deliver value. In this chapter, we will delve into several compelling case studies that highlight AI success stories, showcasing this cutting-edge technology's diverse applications and positive impacts.

One of healthcare's most significant AI success stories revolves around the early detection of diseases. A prominent example is the collaboration between Google Health and Moorfields Eye Hospital in London. AI algorithms were trained on a vast dataset of retinal scans to identify signs of diabetic retinopathy and macular degeneration. The results demonstrated an impressive accuracy rate, enabling quicker diagnosis and intervention, ultimately saving patients from irreversible vision loss.

AI has proven instrumental in fraud detection and risk management in the finance sector. JPMorgan Chase implemented a machine learning system that analyzes vast amounts of financial data in real-time to identify suspicious transactions and patterns indicative of fraudulent activities. This proactive approach has significantly reduced financial losses due to fraud and enhanced the overall security of the banking system.

E-commerce giant Amazon has successfully integrated AI into its operations to enhance the customer experience. The recommendation engine, powered by machine learning algorithms, analyzes user behavior, purchase history, and preferences to suggest products tailored to individual customers. This has increased customer satisfaction and significantly boosted sales and revenue for the company.

Predictive maintenance is a critical application of AI in the manufacturing industry. General Electric (GE) implemented a system that uses sensors and AI algorithms to monitor the performance of industrial machinery. By analyzing data on equipment conditions, the system predicts potential failures before they occur, allowing for timely maintenance and minimizing downtime. This proactive approach has resulted in increased operational efficiency and substantial cost savings.

AI has made significant strides in transforming education by enabling personalized learning experiences. Duolingo, a language learning platform, employs AI algorithms to adapt lessons based on individual proficiency and learning styles. This customized approach has proven effective in improving language acquisition rates, making learning more engaging and accessible for users worldwide.

Precision farming is another area where AI has demonstrated remarkable success. John Deere, a leading agricultural machinery manufacturer, incorporates AI technologies to optimize farming processes. AI-powered systems analyze data from sensors, satellites, and drones to provide farmers with insights into crop health, soil conditions, and weather patterns. This data-driven approach enhances decision-making, leading to increased crop yields and sustainable agriculture practices.

The case studies presented in this chapter highlight the diverse applications of AI across various industries, showcasing the technology's ability to drive innovation, improve efficiency, and deliver tangible benefits. As AI continues to evolve, these success stories serve as inspiration for future advancements and underscore the transformative potential of artificial intelligence in shaping a better and more efficient world.

## Identifying Business Opportunities

Success often hinges on the ability to identify and capitalize on promising opportunities. Recognizing viable business prospects is a crucial skill that can set entrepreneurs and organizations apart. This chapter will explore the multifaceted aspects of identifying business opportunities, from understanding market trends to leveraging emerging technologies.

One of the foundational steps in identifying business opportunities is keeping a keen eye on market trends. Markets constantly evolve, influenced by technological advancements, consumer behavior, and global events. Entrepreneurs and business leaders must conduct thorough market research to discern emerging patterns and shifts.

**Utilizing Data Analytics:** In the digital age, data is a goldmine. Businesses can harness the power of analytics to gain insights into consumer preferences, market gaps, and competitive landscapes. Analyzing data can reveal hidden opportunities and help make informed decisions.

**Staying Customer-Centric:** Understanding the needs and desires of customers is paramount. Conducting surveys focus groups, and analyzing customer feedback can provide valuable information. Businesses aligning their offerings with customer demands often succeed in crowded markets.

Technology is a crucial driver of change, and businesses that embrace technological advancements can uncover unique opportunities. From artificial intelligence and blockchain to the Internet of Things (IoT), emerging technologies open new possibilities for creating innovative products and services.

**Adopting Automation:** Automation can streamline processes, reduce costs, and enhance efficiency. Identifying areas within a business where automation can be applied is a potential opportunity for growth.

**Exploring E-Commerce:** The digital marketplace continues to expand, and businesses can tap into this by exploring e-commerce opportunities. Establishing an online presence or optimizing existing digital platforms can open new markets and revenue streams.

Identifying a niche market or developing a unique value proposition can be a game-changer for businesses. Companies can carve out their space in competitive industries by catering to specific needs or offering something distinct

.

**Researching Untapped Niches:** Thorough research is essential to uncover untapped niches. This involves understanding the pain points of a specific audience and tailoring products or services to meet their unique needs.

Differentiating with Unique Value: Crafting a unique value proposition is crucial. Businesses must communicate what sets them apart from competitors through superior quality, exceptional service, or a novel approach to solving a problem.

Opportunities often arise through connections and collaborations. Networking with other businesses, industry professionals, and potential clients can lead to valuable insights and partnerships. Cultivating Relationships: Building and nurturing relationships with other businesses can lead to mutually beneficial collaborations. Joint ventures, partnerships, and strategic alliances can provide access to new markets, resources, and expertise.

**Attending Industry Events:** Participating in industry conferences, trade shows, and networking events provides opportunities to stay informed about industry trends, connect with key players, and discover potential business openings.

Identifying business opportunities often involves an element of risk. Successful entrepreneurs are willing to take calculated risks and adapt to changing circumstances.

**Encouraging Creativity:** Fostering a culture that encourages employees to think innovatively can lead to identifying novel business opportunities. Companies that empower their workforce to share ideas and take calculated risks are more likely to stay ahead of the curve.

**Agile Decision-Making:** The business landscape is dynamic, and adapting quickly is crucial. Agile decision-making processes allow businesses to respond promptly to changes in the market and capitalize on emerging opportunities.

Identifying business opportunities is an ongoing process that requires a combination of market awareness, technological acumen, networking skills, and a willingness to take risks. Businesses can thrive in a competitive and ever-changing business environment by staying attuned to market trends, embracing innovation, understanding niche markets, building strategic alliances, and maintaining adaptability. In the next chapter, we will delve into the crucial aspects of strategic planning to effectively capitalize on identified opportunities.

# 5. Investing in AI: A Strategic Guide

The world has witnessed an unprecedented surge in the development and integration of artificial intelligence (AI) across various industries. As the transformative power of AI becomes increasingly evident, investors are keen to capitalize on the immense opportunities presented by this technological revolution. This chapter aims to provide a comprehensive strategic guide for investors navigating the complex landscape of AI investments.

Before delving into investment strategies, it is crucial to grasp the diverse landscape of AI. AI encompasses a spectrum of technologies, including machine learning, natural language processing, computer vision, and robotics. Each domain presents unique investment opportunities and challenges, requiring investors to have a nuanced understanding of the sector.

Successful AI investments hinge on identifying key growth areas within the broader AI landscape. Healthcare, finance, manufacturing, and autonomous vehicles have witnessed significant AI-driven advancements. Investors should conduct thorough market research to pinpoint industries where AI applications are poised to make a substantial impact.

In the rapidly evolving field of AI, staying ahead of the competition is paramount. Investors should assess companies' competitive advantages in their portfolio, considering factors such as proprietary algorithms, data access, partnerships, and talent pool. Companies with a robust data infrastructure and a deep understanding of industry-specific challenges will likely have a competitive edge.

AI investments have inherent risks, ranging from ethical concerns to regulatory uncertainties. Investors need to adopt a proactive approach to risk management. This involves staying abreast of regulatory developments, understanding the ethical implications of AI applications, and regularly reassessing investment portfolios to adapt to the industry's dynamic nature.

Diversification remains a fundamental principle in investment strategy, and AI is no exception. Investors should consider diversifying their AI portfolios across different sectors, geographies, and company sizes to mitigate risks associated with market fluctuations and technological uncertainties. Diversification also enables investors to capitalize on emerging opportunities in various niches of the AI ecosystem.

AI investments often require a long-term perspective, as the full potential of AI technologies may take time to unfold. Investors should resist the temptation of short-term gains and instead focus on companies with a sustainable vision, strong fundamentals, and the ability to adapt to evolving market dynamics.

Investing in AI requires a strategic and informed approach, considering the multifaceted nature of the industry. By understanding the AI landscape, identifying growth areas, assessing competitive advantages, managing risks, diversifying portfolios, and adopting a long-term perspective, investors can position themselves to capitalize on the transformative power of artificial intelligence. As AI continues to shape the future of industries worldwide, strategic investments can pave the way for substantial returns and contribute to the ongoing evolution of the global economy.

### Navigating the AI Investment Landscape

The landscape of investment opportunities has undergone a profound transformation with the rise of Artificial Intelligence

(AI). As AI continues to disrupt and reshape industries across the globe, investors are presented with unprecedented opportunities and challenges. Navigating the AI investment landscape requires a nuanced understanding of the technology, market trends, and strategic considerations. This chapter will delve into the critical aspects of AI investment, exploring the diverse avenues, potential risks, and best practices for investors seeking to capitalize on this dynamic and rapidly evolving field.

The first step in navigating the AI investment landscape is understanding the AI ecosystem comprehensively. AI encompasses various technologies, including machine learning, natural language processing, computer vision, and robotics. Investors should be well-versed in the different AI subfields and their applications across healthcare, finance, manufacturing, and more industries.

Machine Learning (ML): ML is the backbone of AI, enabling systems to learn from data and make predictions or decisions. Understanding various ML algorithms and their applications is crucial for assessing investment opportunities.

Natural Language Processing (NLP): NLP empowers machines to understand and generate human language. Investments in chatbots, language translation, and voice recognition technologies fall under this category.

**Computer Vision:** This technology allows machines to interpret and make decisions based on visual data. Investments in autonomous vehicles, facial recognition, and image analysis are part of the computer vision landscape.

**Industry-Specific Applications:** Identify industries with a high potential for AI integration. Healthcare, finance, and e-commerce are examples where AI is driving significant innovation and efficiency.

AI in the Cloud: Cloud-based AI services are gaining popularity, providing scalable and cost-effective business solutions. Investing in cloud service providers offering AI capabilities is a strategic move.

**Edge Computing:** As AI applications become more decentralized, edge computing is emerging as a critical infrastructure. Companies providing edge AI solutions present investment opportunities in this growing market.

Due Diligence: Thoroughly research startups, assessing their technology, leadership, and market positioning. Understand their business models and potential for scalability.

**Partnerships and Collaborations:** Companies that have established partnerships with industry leaders may have a competitive advantage. Evaluate the strength and strategic relevance of these collaborations.

**Diversification:** Larger technology companies often have diverse portfolios. Evaluate the percentage of revenue derived from AI-related activities and assess their commitment to AI innovation.

**Research and Development:** Analyze these companies' AI research and development investments. A solid commitment to advancing AI capabilities signals a long-term strategic vision.

**Ethical Considerations:** Assess the ethical implications of AI technologies. Companies with robust ethical frameworks and responsible AI practices are more likely to navigate regulatory challenges successfully.

**Regulatory Landscape:** Stay informed about the evolving regulatory environment for AI. Compliance with data protection and privacy regulations is crucial for long-term success.

**Cybersecurity:** Recognize the potential cybersecurity risks associated with AI. Invest in companies with robust security measures to protect AI systems from malicious attacks.

Investing in AI requires a holistic understanding of the technology, market dynamics, and potential risks. As AI evolves, staying informed and adapting investment strategies will be crucial to success in the rapidly changing landscape. By embracing the transformative power of AI while remaining vigilant to its challenges, investors can position themselves to capitalize on the unprecedented opportunities that lie ahead.

## Risks and Rewards of AI Investments

Artificial intelligence (AI) has emerged as a transformative force, promising unparalleled advancements across various industries. As businesses seek to capitalize on the potential of AI, investing in this cutting-edge technology has become a strategic imperative. However, with great promise comes great uncertainty. This chapter delves into the risks and rewards associated with AI investments, providing insights to guide investors through the complex terrain of this dynamic field.

AI has the potential to revolutionize business operations, automating repetitive tasks and streamlining processes. Investments in AI can lead to significant gains in efficiency, allowing companies to focus on strategic initiatives and innovation.

Early adopters of AI technologies can gain a competitive edge by leveraging advanced analytics, predictive modeling, and personalized customer experiences. This advantage can translate into increased market share and enhanced brand reputation.

AI investments can save long-term costs by reducing labor costs, minimizing errors, and optimizing resource allocation. The ability of AI to analyze vast datasets quickly can lead to more informed decision-making and resource optimization.

AI systems are designed for scalability, making it easier for businesses to adapt to changing demands. As operations expand, AI can seamlessly scale to handle increased workloads, providing a flexible solution for growing enterprises.

The rapid evolution of AI technology introduces the risk of obsolescence. Investments may become outdated as newer, more advanced solutions emerge. Investors must carefully assess the longevity and adaptability of the chosen AI technologies.

AI relies heavily on data, and the mishandling of sensitive information can lead to severe consequences. Data breaches and privacy violation risks demand robust cybersecurity measures to protect the organization and its stakeholders.

The deployment of AI raises ethical questions regarding bias, transparency, and accountability. Investors must be aware of the potential societal impacts of AI, ensuring that their investments align with ethical standards and regulations.

The legal landscape surrounding AI is continually evolving. Investments must be made with a thorough understanding of existing and forthcoming regulations to mitigate the risk of non-compliance and legal challenges.

Thorough research is paramount before making AI investments. Assess the technological landscape, potential competitors, and the regulatory environment to make informed decisions.

Diversifying AI investments across various technologies and applications can mitigate the risk of dependency on a single solution. This strategy helps balance potential losses with gains from other successful investments.

The dynamic nature of AI requires continuous monitoring of investments. Being agile and adapting to emerging trends ensures that investors stay ahead in the rapidly evolving AI landscape.

Collaboration with industry leaders and forming strategic partnerships can provide valuable insights and reduce risks. Leveraging the expertise of established players in the AI space can enhance the chances of successful investments.

The rewards of AI investments are substantial, but so are the associated risks. Strategic planning, due diligence, and a commitment to ethical practices are essential for navigating the complex landscape of AI investments. As technology continues to shape the future, those who carefully balance risk and reward stand to gain the most from this transformative wave of innovation.

## Building a Diversified AI Portfolio

Individuals and organizations must adopt a strategic approach when building their AI portfolios. One fundamental principle that resonates across successful AI practitioners is the importance of diversification. Like in financial investments, a diversified AI portfolio mitigates risk, enhances adaptability, and ensures sustained innovation. This chapter delves into the nuances of constructing a diversified AI portfolio, covering the selection of diverse AI technologies, applications, and ethical considerations.

The AI ecosystem is multifaceted, comprising various technologies, models, and applications. A narrow focus on a single AI domain may limit the growth potential and expose stakeholders to unforeseen risks. In the context of AI, diversification involves strategically spreading investments across different AI technologies and applications. This hedges against potential failures or setbacks in one area and fosters a comprehensive understanding of AI's capabilities and limitations.

Diversifying the machine learning models within your portfolio is essential for addressing different types of problems. Include supervised learning for labeled data, unsupervised learning for discovering patterns, and reinforcement learning for decision-making scenarios. Additionally, explore emerging models such as transformers and generative adversarial networks (GANs) to stay ahead of technological advancements.

Incorporate NLP applications to enhance communication and interaction. This includes sentiment analysis, chatbots, and language translation. A diversified NLP approach enables you to tackle a broad range of language-related challenges, from customer support automation to multilingual content analysis.

Expand your portfolio with computer vision technologies to process and understand visual information. Object recognition, image classification, and facial recognition are just a few examples. Integrating computer vision into your AI strategy is vital for applications ranging from autonomous vehicles to medical image analysis.

Investing in AI applications for healthcare, such as diagnostic tools, predictive analytics, and personalized medicine, can significantly impact patient outcomes. Diversifying into healthcare applications ensures that your portfolio contributes to societal well-being and business growth.

Financial institutions can benefit from AI applications for fraud detection, algorithmic trading, and risk management. A diversified AI portfolio in the finance sector can lead to increased efficiency, reduced risks, and improved decision-making.

Explore AI applications in education, including intelligent tutoring systems, adaptive learning platforms, and educational content generation. Diversifying into the education sector addresses societal needs and presents opportunities for innovation and collaboration.

While building a diversified AI portfolio, it's imperative to prioritize ethical considerations. Evaluate the potential impact of AI applications on privacy, bias, and job displacement. Actively seek out technologies and applications that align with ethical standards and promote responsible AI development.

A diversified AI portfolio requires active management and continuous adaptation. Stay informed about emerging technologies, market trends, and ethical guidelines. Regularly assess the performance of AI applications, retire outdated models, and introduce new ones to stay at the forefront of innovation.

Building a diversified AI portfolio is a dynamic and strategic process that involves thoughtful consideration of technologies, applications, and ethical implications. By embracing diversity, stakeholders can navigate the evolving AI landscape with resilience, creativity, and a commitment to responsible AI development. In the next chapter, we will delve into the challenges and opportunities of AI implementation in specific industries, providing insights into successful case studies and lessons learned.

# 6. Building Your AI Empire

The rise of artificial intelligence (AI) has ushered in a new era of possibilities and challenges. Building your AI empire requires a strategic approach encompassing vision, resources, and ethical considerations. This chapter will guide you through the essential steps to establish and grow your AI empire.

Begin by clarifying your mission and vision for the AI empire. What problems do you aim to solve? How will your AI solutions benefit society? Define a purpose beyond profit, resonating with your team and potential users.

Research and identify market gaps where AI can make a significant impact. Analyze industries ripe for disruption, considering efficiency, cost-effectiveness, and sustainability. Tailor your AI applications to meet specific needs within these markets.

Building an AI empire demands a multidisciplinary team. Seek machine learning, data science, software engineering, and domain-specific experts. Embrace diversity in thought and background to foster creativity and innovation.

Encourage collaboration and open communication within your team. Establish a culture that values experimentation, learning from failure, and continuous improvement. Foster an environment where every team member feels empowered to contribute ideas.

AI is a rapidly evolving field. Stay informed about the latest breakthroughs, tools, and methodologies. Invest in ongoing training for your team to ensure they remain at the forefront of technological innovation.

Select AI frameworks that align with your goals and your team's skills. Whether it's TensorFlow, PyTorch, or another framework, make informed decisions based on the specific requirements of your projects.

Embed ethical considerations into the fabric of your AI empire. Establish guidelines for responsible AI development, addressing issues like bias, privacy, and transparency. Ensure that your AI applications contribute positively to societal well-being.

Build trust with users, regulators, and the broader community by fostering transparency and engagement. Communicate openly about your AI systems' capabilities, limitations, and potential impact. Seek feedback and iterate on your models to address concerns.

Prepare for growth by investing in scalable infrastructure. Cloud computing, distributed systems, and efficient data storage are vital components to handle the increasing demands of AI applications.

Collaborate with industry partners, research institutions, and startups to leverage collective expertise and resources. Strategic partnerships can accelerate innovation, broaden your reach, and provide access to complementary technologies.

As your AI empire grows, so does the importance of cybersecurity. Protect your AI models, datasets, and infrastructure from potential threats. Implement robust security measures to safeguard against data breaches and unauthorized access.

Stay abreast of evolving regulations in the AI space. Ensure compliance with data protection laws and industry standards. Proactively address potential legal and ethical challenges, positioning your AI empire as a responsible and trustworthy player in the field.

Encourage a mindset of continuous innovation within your AI empire. Allocate resources for research and development to explore emerging technologies and stay ahead of the curve.

Monitor market trends, user feedback, and technological advancements. Be agile and ready to pivot your strategies, ensuring your AI empire remains adaptable and responsive to changing conditions.

Building your AI empire is a dynamic journey that requires a harmonious blend of vision, talent, technology, ethics, and adaptability. By following these guidelines and staying true to your mission, you can lay the foundation for an AI empire that not only thrives in the present but also shapes the future of AI innovation. Remember, the key lies in creating robust AI systems and using them responsibly for the betterment of humanity.

### Developing AI-Driven Products and Services

Integrating artificial intelligence (AI) has become a game-changer for businesses aiming to stay competitive and relevant. Developing AI-driven products and services involves:
- A multidisciplinary approach.
- Combining expertise in data science.
- Software engineering.
- User experience design.
- Domain-specific knowledge.

This chapter explores the key considerations, challenges, and best practices in developing AI-driven solutions.

Before delving into the development process, it is crucial to have a comprehensive understanding of the AI landscape. AI can be broadly categorized into narrow or weak AI and general or strong

AI. Most AI applications today fall under narrow AI, designed to perform specific tasks, such as image recognition, natural language processing, or recommendation systems.

Additionally, the choice between supervised and unsupervised learning is fundamental. In supervised learning, the model is trained on labeled data, while unsupervised learning involves discovering patterns in unlabeled data. Reinforcement learning, where algorithms learn through trial and error, is gaining prominence, particularly in applications like robotics and gaming.

Successful AI development hinges on high-quality data. The saying "garbage in, garbage out" holds in AI. Clean, diverse, and representative datasets are essential for training accurate models. The data should be free from biases that could skew the model's predictions or decisions.

Data privacy and security are critical considerations. Compliance with GDPR (General Data Protection Regulation) or HIPAA (Health Insurance Portability and Accountability Act) is non-negotiable. Implementing robust data governance practices ensures responsible and ethical AI development.

Choosing the suitable AI model depends on the specific problem at hand. Popular frameworks like TensorFlow and PyTorch simplify the development process. Transfer learning, where pre-trained models are fine-tuned for a particular task, can significantly reduce development time and resource requirements.

The model's interpretability is crucial, especially in applications where transparency is essential, such as healthcare or finance. Balancing the trade-off between model complexity and interpretability is an ongoing challenge.

AI development is an iterative process. Continuous testing and validation are necessary to refine models and enhance performance. A/B testing can be employed to compare the effectiveness of different models or algorithms in real-world scenarios.

Addressing issues like overfitting, where a model performs well on training data but needs improvement on new data, is a common challenge. Regular updates and improvements are essential to keep pace with evolving datasets and user needs.

Integrating AI-driven products and services with existing systems requires careful planning. Key considerations include compatibility with legacy systems, scalability, and minimal disruption to current operations. Open APIs (Application Programming Interfaces) and microservices architecture facilitate seamless integration.
Collaboration between data scientists, software engineers, and domain experts is crucial at this stage to ensure a holistic understanding of the organization's needs and challenges.

A user-centric approach is paramount in the development of AI-driven products and services. User experience (UX) design should focus on making AI interactions intuitive, transparent, and valuable for end-users. Clear communication about how AI is being used and what data is collected is essential to build trust. Ethical considerations must be embedded into the development process, including bias mitigation, fairness, and accountability. Regular audits and reviews of AI systems can help identify and address ethical concerns.

Post-deployment, continuous monitoring of AI systems is vital. Monitoring helps detect and address issues such as model drift (changes in input data distribution over time) and performance degradation. Feedback loops should be established to gather end-user insights, enabling continuous improvement.

Regular maintenance, updates, and patches are essential to address security vulnerabilities, improve model accuracy, and adapt to evolving user requirements.

Developing AI-driven products and services is a dynamic and multifaceted process that requires collaboration across disciplines. Organizations that successfully navigate the challenges and embrace ethical AI principles stand to gain a competitive edge in delivering innovative solutions. As AI advances, staying abreast of the latest developments and incorporating feedback loops into the development lifecycle will be crucial for long-term success.

One of the critical stages is the selection and training of machine learning models. This process lays the foundation for the intelligence and capabilities of the final product. This chapter will explore the key considerations, methodologies, and best practices associated with model selection and training.

Machine learning model selection is a pivotal decision that significantly influences an AI-driven product's performance, efficiency, and adaptability. It involves choosing an appropriate algorithm or architecture tailored to the specific problem. The selection process should consider the data's nature, the problem's complexity, and the desired outcomes.

**Supervised Learning Models:** These models are trained on labeled data, where the algorithm learns to map input features to corresponding output labels. Standard algorithms include linear regression, support vector machines, and neural networks.

**Unsupervised Learning Models:** Operating on unlabeled data, these models discover patterns and relationships within the data. Examples include clustering algorithms like K-means, hierarchical clustering, and dimensionality reduction techniques like principal component analysis (PCA).

Reinforcement Learning Models: These models learn by interacting with an environment and receiving feedback as rewards. Reinforcement learning is often used in scenarios where an agent makes sequential decisions.

**Data Characteristics:** Understand the nature of your data, including its size, distribution, and potential biases. Different algorithms perform better on certain types of data.

**Model Complexity:** Balance the complexity of the model with the available data. Overly complex models might overfit the training data, while straightforward models may not capture the underlying patterns.

**Scalability:** Consider the scalability of the chosen model. Will it be able to handle larger datasets or increased computational demands as the product evolves?

Once a suitable model is selected, the training process begins. This involves exposing the model to labeled data, allowing it to adjust its parameters and internal representations to make accurate predictions or decisions. Proper training is crucial for achieving high-performance AI-driven products.

Before training a model, it's essential to preprocess the data. This includes handling missing values, scaling features, and encoding categorical variables. Proper preprocessing ensures that the model can effectively learn from the input data.

**Splitting the Data:** Divide the dataset into training, validation, and test sets. Training data is used to train the model, validation data helps tune hyperparameters, and the test set evaluates the model's performance on unseen data.

Hyperparameter Tuning: Experiment with different hyperparameter settings to optimize the model's performance.

Techniques such as grid search or random search can be employed.

**Regularization:** Introduce regularization techniques to prevent overfitting. Standard methods include L1 and L2 regularization, dropout in neural networks, and early stopping during training. After training, evaluate the model's performance using metrics relevant to the problem (e.g., accuracy, precision, recall, F1 score). If the model does not meet the desired criteria, iterate by adjusting hyperparameters, trying different algorithms, or collecting additional data.

The development of AI-driven products continues after the initial model deployment. Continuous learning and model maintenance are integral for adapting to changing environments, user behavior, and data patterns.

Implement robust monitoring systems to track the model's performance in real-world scenarios. Establish feedback loops that allow the model to learn from new data and adapt over time. As the product evolves, it may be necessary to update the model. Implement versioning mechanisms to keep track of changes and ensure a seamless transition when deploying updated models.

Throughout the model selection and training process, be mindful of ethical considerations. Address potential biases in the data, ensure transparency in decision-making, and prioritize fairness and accountability.

To illustrate the concepts discussed in this chapter, let's consider the development of a movie recommender system. We'll explore how different model selection and training strategies impact the system's performance and user satisfaction.

**Collaborative Filtering:** This approach recommends movies based on user preferences and similarities with other users.

Popular algorithms include user-based and item-based collaborative filtering.

**Content-Based Filtering:** This approach recommends movies based on the characteristics of the films and the user's preferences. It involves analyzing features such as genre, actors, and directors.

**Data Preprocessing:** Handle missing values, scale numerical features, and encode categorical variables. For collaborative filtering, create user-item interaction matrices.

**Training Pipeline:** Split the data into training and validation sets. Experiment with different hyperparameters, such as the number of latent factors in collaborative filtering or the weight assigned to other features in content-based filtering.

**Evaluation and Iteration:** Use metrics like Mean Squared Error (MSE) or precision at k to evaluate the model's performance. Iterate by adjusting hyperparameters, incorporating user feedback, and retraining the model.

**Monitoring:** Implement a monitoring system to track user interactions with the recommender system. Monitor changes in user preferences and adapt the model accordingly.

**Feedback Loops:** Allow users to provide feedback on recommendations. Use this feedback to improve the model and continuously enhance user satisfaction.

In developing AI-driven products and services, carefully selecting and training machine learning models are pivotal to success. This chapter has provided an in-depth exploration of the considerations, methodologies, and best practices associated with model selection and training. By understanding these principles and incorporating them into the development process, practitioners can create intelligent, adaptive, and ethically sound

AI-driven solutions that meet the needs of users and stakeholders alike.

Integrating Artificial Intelligence (AI) into existing products has become a pivotal strategy for companies seeking to stay competitive and meet the ever-changing demands of consumers. This chapter explores the nuances and challenges of integrating AI into established products, focusing on the development of AI-driven products and services.

Integrating AI into existing products is not merely a technological upgrade but a strategic imperative. Businesses across industries recognize the potential of AI to enhance functionality, improve user experience, and unlock new possibilities. AI can revolutionize how products and services are conceived, delivered, and consumed in manufacturing, healthcare, finance, or entertainment.

Before embarking on the integration journey, companies must assess their readiness. This involves evaluating the current state of technology infrastructure, workforce skills, and organizational culture. The integration of AI requires a collaborative effort between technical and non-technical teams, necessitating a cultural shift towards embracing data-driven decision-making.

Selecting the appropriate AI model is a critical decision. Depending on the nature of the product or service, companies may opt for machine learning algorithms, natural language processing, computer vision, or a combination of these. The choice must align with the specific goals and challenges of the integration, ensuring that the AI system adds tangible value to the existing product.

The backbone of any AI system is data. Integrating AI into existing products requires a seamless integration of relevant datasets. Companies must establish robust data pipelines, ensuring that the AI models have access to high-quality, diverse data. Simultaneously, data security measures must be prioritized to safeguard sensitive information, comply with industry regulations, and protect user privacy.

Successful integration hinges on effective collaboration between AI systems and human users. User interfaces must be designed with simplicity and intuitiveness, enabling users to interact seamlessly with the AI-powered features. Furthermore, companies should invest in user education to foster understanding and trust in AI, promoting a positive user experience.

Despite the immense potential, integrating AI into existing products has its share of challenges. These include legacy system compatibility, ethical considerations, and the potential impact on the workforce. Companies must proactively address these challenges through careful planning, transparent communication, and reskilling initiatives to empower employees with the skills required for the AI-driven future.

Examining real-world case studies provides valuable insights into the dos and don'ts of AI integration. Success stories from various industries illustrate the transformative power of AI, while lessons learned highlight common pitfalls and how they can be avoided. Learning from the experiences of others accelerates the integration process and increases the likelihood of positive outcomes.

Integrating AI into existing products is not a one-time endeavor but an ongoing process. Companies must embrace a culture of continuous improvement and adaptation. Regular updates, feedback loops, and monitoring mechanisms should be established to ensure that the AI remains relevant, efficient, and aligned with the evolving needs of users and the market.

As technology continues to advance, the integration of AI into existing products will become increasingly sophisticated. The future promises AI-powered products that seamlessly adapt to user preferences, anticipate needs and contribute to a more personalized and efficient user experience. Staying at the forefront of AI integration is a strategic advantage and a necessity for companies aspiring to lead in the digital era.

Integrating AI into existing products is a complex yet essential endeavor for businesses aiming to thrive in a data-driven world. By understanding the imperative, assessing readiness, choosing the suitable AI model, prioritizing data integration and security, fostering human-machine collaboration, overcoming challenges, learning from case studies, embracing continuous improvement, and looking ahead to the future, companies can navigate the intricacies of AI integration and unlock new possibilities for innovation and growth.

In the development lifecycle of AI-driven products and services, testing and deployment are critical phases that ensure the developed solutions' reliability, performance, and effectiveness. This chapter explores the key considerations, methodologies, and best practices in testing and deploying AI products.

Unit testing in AI development focuses on individual components of the model, such as specific functions or algorithms. Developers create test cases to verify that each code unit produces the expected output. This helps identify and rectify errors in the early stages of development.

Integration testing evaluates the interactions between different components of the AI system. This ensures that various modules work seamlessly together. The goal is to detect any issues that may arise when combining other aspects of the system.

Performance testing assesses how well an AI model performs under different conditions. It involves measuring response times, resource usage, and scalability. Rigorous performance testing helps optimize the model for efficiency and responsiveness.

Robustness testing evaluates the AI model's ability to handle unexpected inputs, outliers, and adverse conditions. This ensures that the model remains reliable and accurate in real-world scenarios.

Given the sensitive nature of many AI applications, security testing is paramount. This involves identifying and addressing potential vulnerabilities in the system, protecting against data breaches, and ensuring compliance with privacy regulations.

A/B testing involves deploying two versions of the AI model concurrently—version A (the existing model) and version B (the updated model). This allows for directly comparing their performance in a real-world environment, helping developers make informed decisions about the new model's effectiveness.

Canary releases involve gradually rolling out a new AI model to a subset of users before deploying it to the entire user base. This incremental approach allows developers to monitor the model's performance and user feedback, reducing the risk of widespread issues.

Two identical environments (blue and green) are maintained in blue-green deployments. The current production version runs in one environment (e.g., blue), while the updated version is deployed in another (green). Switching between environments is seamless, providing a quick rollback option if issues arise.

Continuous monitoring is crucial for the long-term success of AI products. This involves tracking the model's performance, user feedback, and data drift. Regular updates and maintenance ensure the model remains accurate and aligns with evolving user needs.

Throughout the testing and deployment phases, ethical considerations must be prioritized. This includes addressing training data biases, ensuring AI decision-making transparency, and adhering to ethical guidelines and regulations.

Testing and deploying AI products require a meticulous approach to ensure reliability, security, and user satisfaction. By incorporating comprehensive testing strategies and thoughtful deployment practices, developers can deliver AI-driven products and services that meet high performance and ethical responsibility standards.

## Creating a Startup in the AI Space

Artificial intelligence (AI) stands out as a transformative force, reshaping industries, businesses, and daily life. As an entrepreneur, venturing into AI offers unprecedented opportunities and challenges. This chapter delves into the intricacies of creating a startup in the AI domain, providing a roadmap for aspiring innovators.

Before embarking on your entrepreneurial journey, it's crucial to comprehend the diverse facets of the AI landscape. AI encompasses machine learning, natural language processing, computer vision, and more. Identify specific niches or problems within these domains where your startup can make a meaningful impact. Consider areas like healthcare, finance, cybersecurity, or automation, depending on your expertise and interests.

AI startups thrive on technical prowess. Assemble a multidisciplinary team with machine learning, data science, and software engineering expertise. Diverse perspectives foster innovation, and a skilled team can navigate the complexities of AI development.

Conduct extensive market research to validate your startup idea. Understand your target audience, analyze competitors, and identify gaps in the market. This information will shape your product development and market strategy.

Given the ethical concerns and data privacy issues, navigating the legal landscape is crucial in AI. Consult legal experts to ensure compliance with regulations and intellectual property protection.

Adopt an MVP (Minimum Viable Product) approach to test your ideas quickly and gather user feedback. Iterate based on this feedback to refine your product. The agile methodology is particularly effective in the fast-paced AI environment.

Data is the lifeblood of AI. Develop robust data collection and preprocessing pipelines to ensure the quality and relevance of your training data. Leverage both proprietary and publicly available datasets.

Invest time and resources in training and validating your AI models. Rigorous testing ensures that your product performs reliably and ethically. Consider partnering with experts to validate your models' fairness and mitigate biases.

AI development often requires substantial resources. Explore funding options, including venture capital, government grants, and strategic partnerships. Clearly articulate the value proposition of your AI solution to attract investors.

Utilize cloud services to scale your AI infrastructure efficiently. Platforms like AWS, Azure, and Google Cloud offer powerful tools for AI development, reducing the need for extensive upfront investments.

Plan for scalability from the outset. AI startups can experience rapid growth, and a scalable infrastructure ensures smooth expansion. Monitor performance metrics and optimize your system accordingly.

Explore monetization strategies like subscription models, licensing, or usage-based pricing. Tailor your approach to your target market and the unique value proposition your AI solution provides.

Prioritize ethical considerations in AI development. Implement responsible AI practices, including transparency, accountability, and user consent. Proactively address biases and ensure that your technology aligns with societal values.

Educate your customers about the capabilities and limitations of your AI solution. Establish clear communication channels to address concerns and build trust.

The AI landscape is evolving rapidly. Stay informed about the latest advancements, and be prepared to adapt your product and strategies accordingly. Foster a culture of continuous learning within your team.

Launching a startup in the AI space is a challenging yet rewarding endeavor. By understanding the intricacies of AI, building a solid foundation, and navigating ethical considerations, you can position your startup for success. Embrace innovation, stay agile, and contribute to the transformative power of artificial intelligence in shaping the future.

## Scaling Your AI Business

Scaling an artificial intelligence (AI) business presents a unique set of challenges and opportunities. As your company grows, so do the complexities associated with managing resources, expanding your customer base, and staying at the forefront of technological advancements. This chapter will explore critical strategies for scaling your AI business effectively.

Successful scaling begins with a robust infrastructure and technology stack. Ensure that your AI algorithms and models are designed for scalability. Consider leveraging cloud services to handle increased computational demands. Cloud platforms like AWS, Azure, or Google Cloud offer scalable solutions that can grow with your business.

Investing in automation tools, DevOps practices, and containerization can streamline your development and deployment processes, enabling you to respond rapidly to changing demands.
Scaling your AI business requires a skilled and agile team.

Attracting top talent is crucial, so focus on recruiting individuals with machine learning, data science, and software engineering expertise. Foster a culture of continuous learning by providing training opportunities for your existing team to stay updated on the latest advancements in AI technology.

Collaborate with educational institutions and participate in industry events to create a pipeline of fresh talent and maintain strong connections with the academic community.

As your AI business expands, the volume of data you handle will grow exponentially. Implement robust data management and governance practices to ensure data quality, security, and compliance. Establish precise data collection, storage, and processing protocols, and stay informed about data privacy regulations that may impact your operations.

Consider implementing AI-driven solutions for data management, such as automated data labeling and cleaning tools, to enhance efficiency and accuracy.

Prioritize customer success and support as an integral part of your scaling strategy. As you acquire new customers, focus on delivering a seamless onboarding experience and provide responsive customer support. Develop a comprehensive knowledge base and self-service resources to empower users and reduce the burden on your support team.

Leverage AI technologies like chatbots and virtual assistants to automate routine customer interactions and free up resources for more complex issues.

Scaling your AI business may involve expanding into new markets. Consider the cultural and linguistic nuances of different regions when deploying AI solutions. Invest in localization efforts to adapt your products and services to the specific needs of diverse customer bases.

Build strategic partnerships with local businesses and explore collaborations with international experts to gain insights into regional preferences and regulations.

Commit to continuous innovation and research to stay com:
1. Commit to the rapidly evolving AI landscape.
2. llocate resources for R&D projects that explore cutting-edge technologies and emerging trends.

Oster a culture of experimentation and encourage your team to explore new ideas, keeping your business ahead of the curve.
1.

 Actively engage with the broader AI community, attend conferences, and participate in open-source initiatives to stay informed about the latest breakthroughs and collaborate with other innovators.

Scaling your AI business is a dynamic and multifaceted process that requires careful planning and execution. By investing in the right technology, nurturing a talented team, and prioritizing customer success, you can navigate growth challenges and position your business for long-term success in the rapidly advancing field of artificial intelligence.

## 7. AI and Personal Finance

Artificial Intelligence (AI) has emerged as a transformative force, reshaping how individuals manage, invest, and plan their financial futures. This chapter explores the profound impact of AI on personal finance, examining its applications, benefits, challenges, and the future outlook for this dynamic intersection.

Personal Budgeting and Expense Tracking:
AI has revolutionized the way individuals budget and track expenses. Advanced algorithms analyze spending patterns, identify trends, and offer personalized insights to help users make informed decisions. AI-driven budgeting apps can provide real-time updates, predict future expenditures, and recommend adjustments to meet financial goals.

Automated Financial Advice:
Robo-advisors, powered by AI, have gained popularity in offering automated, low-cost investment advice. These platforms leverage algorithms to assess risk tolerance, financial goals, and market conditions, providing tailored investment portfolios. The accessibility and affordability of robo-advisors democratize investment management, making it accessible to a broader audience.

Enhanced Credit Scoring:
Traditional credit scoring models are often limited in assessing an individual's creditworthiness. AI algorithms incorporate many data points, including non-traditional sources such as social media

behavior and online transactions, to generate more accurate and comprehensive credit scores. This enables lenders to make more informed decisions and extends credit to individuals with limited credit histories.

Algorithmic Lending:
AI-driven lending platforms streamline the loan approval process. These platforms leverage machine learning to analyze vast datasets quickly, assess risk, and determine suitable interest rates. Borrowers benefit from faster approval times and more competitive loan terms, while lenders mitigate risks through advanced risk assessment models.

Advanced Fraud Detection:
AI plays a pivotal role in enhancing the security of personal finance. Machine learning algorithms analyze transaction patterns and user behavior to detect anomalies indicative of fraudulent activity. Real-time alerts and proactive measures help prevent unauthorized access, protecting individuals from financial fraud.

Biometric Authentication:
AI-driven biometric authentication methods, such as facial recognition and fingerprint scanning, add more security to financial transactions. These technologies enhance security and streamline the user experience by reducing reliance on traditional authentication methods like passwords.

Data Privacy Concerns:
Integrating AI in personal finance raises concerns about the privacy of sensitive financial data. Striking a balance between harnessing the power of AI and safeguarding individual privacy requires robust regulations, transparent policies, and secure data handling practices.

AI algorithms are only as unbiased as the data they are trained on. If historical data contains biases, AI systems may perpetuate and amplify those biases. Addressing algorithmic bias in personal finance is crucial to ensuring fair and equitable financial services for all.

Personalized Financial Planning:
The future of AI in personal finance holds the promise of even more personalized and proactive financial planning. As AI algorithms evolve, they will provide increasingly accurate predictions, recommend tailored strategies, and empower individuals to achieve their financial goals more effectively.

Integration of Blockchain and AI:
Integrating blockchain technology with AI could further enhance personal finance's security, transparency, and efficiency. Smart contracts, powered by AI and blockchain, may redefine how financial agreements are executed, providing a decentralized and tamper-resistant framework.

The marriage of AI and personal finance has ushered in an era of unprecedented innovation and efficiency. While presenting immense opportunities for financial empowerment, it also necessitates careful consideration of ethical implications and regulatory frameworks. As we navigate this transformative landscape, the collaboration between technology developers, financial institutions, and regulators will be crucial in ensuring a future where AI is a powerful tool for improving individual economic well-being.

## AI in Personal Investing

Artificial intelligence (AI) has emerged as a transformative force, reshaping how individuals manage their finances and make investment decisions. This chapter delves into the various facets of AI in personal investing, exploring its impact, benefits, and potential challenges.

Traditionally, personal investing requires a significant amount of time and expertise. Investors relied on financial advisors, historical market data, and their intuition to navigate the complexities of the financial markets. However, with the advent of AI, the dynamics of personal investing have undergone a radical transformation.

AI, particularly machine learning algorithms, has proven to be a game-changer in predicting market trends and analyzing vast datasets. These algorithms can process and interpret information at speeds unimaginable for humans, identifying patterns, correlations, and anomalies that may elude the human eye. This enables investors to make more informed decisions based on data-driven insights.

The rise of robo-advisors exemplifies the integration of AI in personal investing. These digital platforms leverage algorithms to create and manage diversified portfolios tailored to individual investors' risk tolerance, financial goals, and time horizons. The accessibility and cost-effectiveness of robo-advisors have democratized investing, allowing individuals with varying levels of financial literacy to participate in the markets.

Social media platforms are crucial in shaping market sentiment in the information age. AI-powered sentiment analysis tools sift through vast amounts of social media data, news articles, and online discussions to gauge public sentiment about specific stocks, industries, or the market as a whole. Investors can leverage this information to stay ahead of market trends and anticipate potential market movements.

AI has significantly enhanced risk management in personal investing. Advanced algorithms can analyze an individual's risk profile, assess the risk associated with specific investments, and dynamically adjust portfolios to align with changing market conditions. Additionally, AI is instrumental in fraud detection, helping safeguard investors from malicious activities in the increasingly digital financial landscape.

While AI brings about numerous benefits in personal investing, it is not without its challenges. The potential for algorithmic biases, data privacy concerns, and the risk of over-reliance on technology are important considerations. Striking a balance between the human touch and the efficiency of AI remains a critical aspect of ethical personal investing.

As technology advances, AI's future in personal investing holds exciting possibilities. Quantum computing, improved natural language processing, and increased integration of AI with blockchain technology are expected to enhance investment strategies' accuracy and efficiency. Additionally, ethical frameworks and regulations will likely evolve to ensure responsible AI use in the financial industry.

AI has ushered in a new era of personal investing, empowering individuals with sophisticated tools and insights that were once exclusive to institutional investors. While challenges persist, the potential for AI to optimize investment decision-making and democratize access to financial markets is undeniable. As the intersection of finance and technology evolves, personal investors are poised to navigate the markets with unprecedented precision and confidence.

## Automating Financial Decision-Making

The integration of technology has revolutionized the way decisions are made. Automation, in particular, has emerged as a powerful tool in streamlining and enhancing financial decision-making processes. This chapter delves into the various facets of automating financial decision-making, exploring its benefits, challenges, and transformative impact on businesses and individuals.

Automation in financial decision-making refers to using technology and algorithms to execute tasks traditionally performed by humans. This trend has gained momentum as advancements in artificial intelligence (AI), machine learning (ML), and data analytics have made it possible to process vast amounts of financial data with unprecedented speed and accuracy.

**Efficiency and Speed:** One of the primary advantages of automating financial decision-making is the significant boost in efficiency and speed. Algorithms can analyze large datasets in real-time, enabling rapid decision-making processes surpassing human capabilities.

**Accuracy and Consistency:** Automation minimizes the risk of human error inherent in financial tasks. Algorithms consistently apply predefined rules and criteria, reducing the likelihood of miscalculations or oversights. This heightened accuracy contributes to more reliable economic outcomes.

**Cost Savings:** Organizations benefit from cost savings by reducing manual labor and the associated expenses. Automation allows for optimizing resource allocation, freeing personnel to focus on more complex and strategic aspects of financial management.

**Algorithmic Trading:** Automated trading systems use algorithms to execute buy or sell orders in financial markets. These systems leverage real-time market data and historical trends to make split-second trading decisions, often outperforming human traders in speed and precision.

**Credit Scoring:** Financial institutions employ automated credit scoring models to assess the creditworthiness of individuals and businesses. To automate lending decisions, these models consider various factors, including credit history, income, and debt levels.

**Robo-Advisors:** Automated investment platforms, known as robo-advisors, use algorithms to create and manage investment portfolios. These platforms assess an investor's risk tolerance, financial goals, and market conditions to make investment decisions on their behalf.

While the benefits of automating financial decision-making are compelling, some challenges and considerations must be addressed to ensure responsible and effective implementation. As financial data becomes more digitized, robust security measures are paramount. Protecting sensitive financial information from cyber threats and unauthorized access is crucial to maintaining the trust of both individuals and organizations.

Automated decision-making raises ethical questions, especially regarding issues like bias in algorithms. If historical data used to train algorithms contains biases, it may result in discriminatory outcomes. Striking a balance between efficiency and fairness is an ongoing challenge.

The financial industry is subject to stringent regulations to safeguard consumers' interests and maintain the financial system's stability. Implementing automated systems requires adherence to these regulations, necessitating ongoing monitoring and adaptation to evolving compliance standards.
As technology continues to advance, the future of automated financial decision-making holds exciting possibilities.
The synergy between AI and human expertise will likely define the characteristics of the future. While automation can handle routine and data-intensive tasks, human judgment, creativity, and ethical considerations will remain essential in complex decision-making scenarios.

Innovation in automation technologies, including developing more sophisticated algorithms and AI models, will continuously improve financial decision-making processes. Financial institutions and businesses that embrace and adapt to these innovations will maintain a competitive edge.

Automation is not limited to institutional use; individuals increasingly leverage automated tools for personal finance. From budgeting and savings to investment management, automated solutions empower individuals to make informed financial decisions in their daily lives.

Automating financial decision-making represents a paradigm shift in how businesses and individuals navigate the complex world of finance. The benefits of efficiency, accuracy, and cost savings are undeniable, but the challenges of data security, ethical considerations, and regulatory compliance cannot be ignored. Striking the right balance between automation and human oversight is critical to unlocking the full potential of this transformative technology. As we move into the future, the evolution of automated financial decision-making will undoubtedly shape the economic landscape in ways we are only beginning to imagine.

## Smart Wealth Management with AI

Artificial intelligence (AI) integration has revolutionized how individuals manage their wealth. Smart Wealth Management powered by AI has emerged as a game-changer, offering unprecedented insights, efficiency, and personalized strategies for financial success. In this chapter, we delve into the intricacies of

Smart Wealth Management and explore how AI is reshaping the future of economic well-being.

Smart Wealth Management refers to using advanced technologies, particularly AI and machine learning, to optimize and automate the processes involved in financial planning, investment, and overall wealth management. This approach leverages algorithms that analyze vast data, providing users with tailored advice, risk assessments, and investment strategies.

AI excels at processing and analyzing large datasets. Wealth management platforms utilize this capability to scrutinize historical financial data, market trends, and economic indicators. By employing predictive modeling, AI algorithms can identify patterns and make informed forecasts, assisting investors in making strategic decisions.

One of the critical advantages of Smart Wealth Management is its ability to create personalized financial plans. AI algorithms consider individual goals, risk tolerance, income, and expenses to craft customized plans that align with users' unique circumstances.

Gone are the days of manual portfolio adjustments. AI-powered wealth management systems continuously monitor portfolios, rebalance assets, and optimize investment strategies based on market conditions. This automation ensures that portfolios are aligned with users' goals while adapting to changing financial landscapes.

AI algorithms assess risk by considering factors such as market volatility, economic indicators, and geopolitical events. Wealth management platforms leverage this capability to provide real-time risk assessments, enabling investors to make informed decisions that align with their risk tolerance.

AI analyzes vast amounts of market data, identifying emerging trends and opportunities. Wealth management platforms equipped with AI offer users valuable insights into market dynamics, helping them stay ahead of the curve and make timely investment decisions.

While Smart Wealth Management with AI presents numerous benefits, it has challenges. Security concerns, algorithmic biases, and the need for ongoing user education are among the considerations that must be addressed to ensure the responsible and effective use of AI in wealth management.

As AI technology advances, the future of Smart Wealth Management holds excellent promise. Improved algorithms, enhanced data security measures, and increased integration with other emerging technologies, such as blockchain, are expected to further elevate the capabilities of AI in reshaping the landscape of wealth management.

Smart Wealth Management with AI is ushering in a new era of financial empowerment. By harnessing the power of artificial intelligence, individuals can make more informed decisions, optimize their economic strategies, and ultimately achieve their health-related goals. As technology continues to evolve, the marriage of AI and wealth management is set to redefine how we navigate the complexities of the financial world.

## 8. Ethical Considerations in AI Wealth Creation

The intersection with wealth creation brings forth a host of ethical considerations that demand careful examination. As AI technologies advance and permeate various industries, their impact on wealth generation becomes increasingly pronounced. This chapter delves into the ethical dimensions of AI-driven wealth creation, addressing key concerns and proposing guidelines for a responsible and equitable approach.

The surge in AI-driven wealth creation raises fundamental questions about the distribution of benefits and potential societal disparities. As we navigate this landscape, it is imperative to prioritize ethical considerations to ensure that the benefits of AI are accessible, inclusive, and aligned with broader societal values.

One of the foremost ethical concerns in AI wealth creation is the perpetuation of bias. AI systems, often trained on historical data, can inherit and perpetuate societal biases. In the context of wealth creation, this bias can lead to exclusionary practices, reinforcing existing inequalities. Developers and policymakers must adopt strategies to identify and rectify biases in AI algorithms, ensuring fair and equitable wealth distribution.

Transparency is critical in fostering trust between AI systems and society. Lack of transparency in the algorithms that underpin wealth creation can result in suspicion and resistance. Developers should prioritize openness, providing clear explanations of AI decision-making processes. Additionally, establishing accountability mechanisms ensures that stakeholders can address the consequences of AI-generated wealth and hold responsible parties accountable for any adverse outcomes.

AI-driven wealth creation should not inadvertently exacerbate existing disparities. Ensuring accessibility and inclusivity means addressing barriers that could impede certain groups from benefiting. This involves proactive efforts to bridge the digital divide, provide education and training opportunities, and actively include diverse perspectives in developing and deploying AI systems.

The rapid integration of AI in wealth creation may lead to job displacement and economic disruption. Ethical considerations must extend to mitigating these impacts. Initiatives such as reskilling and upskilling programs can help affected workers transition into new roles, ensuring that the benefits of AI are not achieved at the expense of widespread unemployment.

AI systems often rely on vast amounts of data, raising concerns about privacy and security. Safeguarding individuals' data is paramount to ethical AI wealth creation. Robust data protection measures, precise consent mechanisms, and strict adherence to privacy regulations are essential to prevent unauthorized access and misuse of personal information.

The computational demands of AI can have environmental implications. Ethical considerations extend to minimizing AI systems' ecological footprint in wealth creation. This involves adopting energy-efficient algorithms, exploring renewable energy sources for computing infrastructure, and promoting sustainability in developing and deploying AI technologies.

Given the global nature of AI and its impact on wealth creation, ethical considerations should be addressed collaboratively on an international scale. Establishing ethical frameworks, standards, and governance mechanisms that transcend borders is essential to promote responsible AI practices and prevent unethical exploitation.

Ethical considerations in AI wealth creation demand ongoing attention and a proactive approach. Balancing innovation with social responsibility requires a commitment from developers, policymakers, and stakeholders to prioritize fairness, transparency, inclusivity, and sustainability. By adhering to these ethical principles, we can ensure that AI-driven wealth creation contributes positively to society, fostering a future where the benefits of technological advancement are shared equitably.

## Addressing Bias in AI Systems

The rapid integration of artificial intelligence (AI) into various sectors has undeniably revolutionized how we live, work, and interact. One of the key areas where AI has made a significant impact is wealth creation. As AI systems play a crucial role in financial markets, investment strategies, and economic decision-making, addressing the ethical considerations surrounding bias in AI systems is imperative. This chapter delves into the challenges and solutions associated with mitigating bias in AI systems within the context of honest wealth creation.

Bias in AI systems refers to unfair and discriminatory outcomes that may result from the data used to train these systems. In the realm of wealth creation, biases in AI can have profound consequences, exacerbating existing inequalities and perpetuating systemic issues. These biases can emerge from various sources, including historical data, socio-economic disparities, and institutional practices.

AI systems often learn from historical data, which may reflect and perpetuate societal biases. For example, suppose historical financial data exhibits gender or racial biases. In that case, AI systems trained on such data may inadvertently reinforce these biases when making predictions or decisions related to wealth creation.

AI systems may also inherit socio-economic biases embedded in the data they are trained on. This can reinforce existing wealth gaps, as the algorithms may favor certain groups over others, perpetuating systemic inequalities.

The practices and policies of institutions deploying AI systems can introduce biases. For instance, if an investment firm has historically favored certain demographic groups, the AI models developed by that firm may replicate and amplify these biases unless proactive measures are taken.

To mitigate bias, it is essential to ensure that AI systems are trained on diverse and representative datasets. This involves actively seeking out and incorporating data from a wide range of sources to avoid the perpetuation of existing biases.

Transparency in the design and operation of AI algorithms is crucial for understanding and addressing biases. Developers and stakeholders can identify and rectify biases more effectively by making algorithms more interpretable.

Establishing ethical frameworks and oversight mechanisms for AI deployment in wealth creation is essential. This includes creating guidelines that prioritize fairness, accountability, and transparency. Independent oversight bodies can ensure adherence to these principles.

AI systems must be subject to continuous monitoring and updating to adapt to evolving societal norms and values. Regular audits of AI models can identify and rectify biases that may emerge over time.

As AI continues to shape the landscape of wealth creation, addressing bias in AI systems is paramount for ensuring ethical and equitable outcomes. By understanding the sources of bias and implementing proactive measures, stakeholders can contribute to developing AI systems that promote inclusivity, fairness, and responsible wealth creation. This chapter has outlined vital considerations and strategies to guide practitioners, policymakers, and researchers in navigating the complex terrain of bias in AI for ethical wealth creation.

## Ensuring Fairness and Accountability

Ethical considerations play a pivotal role in shaping the trajectory of technological advancements. As society embraces the transformative power of AI, it becomes imperative to safeguard against potential pitfalls, ensuring that wealth creation through these technologies is robust but also fair and accountable. This chapter delves into the ethical considerations surrounding AI-driven wealth creation, emphasizing the need for fairness, transparency, and accountability.

One of the fundamental ethical concerns in AI wealth creation lies in the fairness of algorithms. As AI systems analyze vast amounts of data to make decisions, they can inadvertently perpetuate and amplify existing biases. For instance, biased algorithms in financial systems may disadvantage specific demographics, reinforcing societal inequalities. To address this, developers and policymakers must prioritize developing fair and unbiased algorithms that promote inclusivity.

Developers must adopt strategies to identify and mitigate bias in AI algorithms. This involves continuous monitoring, auditing, and refining of algorithms to ensure they treat all individuals fairly, regardless of race, gender, or socioeconomic background. Additionally, incorporating diverse perspectives within development teams can help uncover and rectify biases that might go unnoticed.

Another critical aspect of ethical AI wealth creation is transparency. As AI algorithms make decisions that impact financial outcomes, it is crucial to provide users with a clear understanding of the underlying processes. Transparent AI systems build trust among users and empower them to make informed decisions.

The concept of Explainable AI (XAI) is gaining prominence, especially in financial applications. XAI ensures that the decision-making process of AI algorithms is interpretable by humans. This transparency allows users to comprehend how AI systems arrive at specific conclusions, enhancing accountability and mitigating concerns related to some advanced algorithms' "black box" nature.

Accountability is a cornerstone of ethical AI. Establishing accountability mechanisms ensures stakeholders are held responsible for the consequences of AI-driven wealth creation. This accountability extends to developers, organizations deploying AI systems, and policymakers shaping the regulatory landscape.

The AI community must work collectively to establish ethical frameworks and standards to promote accountability. These frameworks should guide the responsible development and deployment of AI technologies, emphasizing the importance of fairness, transparency, and the overall societal impact of these systems.

Government and regulatory bodies are pivotal in ensuring accountability in AI wealth creation. Developing and enforcing regulations that mandate ethical considerations, auditing processes, and penalties for non-compliance are essential in creating a responsible AI ecosystem.

Collaboration between governments, industry leaders, academia, and advocacy groups is crucial in establishing effective governance models. By working together, stakeholders can create policies that balance innovation with ethical considerations, fostering an environment where AI-driven wealth creation aligns with societal values.

As AI continues to shape the landscape of wealth creation, ensuring fairness and accountability is paramount. By addressing biases, promoting transparency, and establishing robust accountability mechanisms, we can harness the transformative power of AI to create wealth in a manner that benefits society as a whole. Ethical considerations should guide every step of the AI development and deployment process, ensuring that the benefits of wealth creation are shared equitably and responsibly across diverse communities.

## The Role of AI in a Sustainable Future

The integration of Artificial Intelligence (AI) has emerged as a powerful force with the potential to reshape economies, industries, and societies. As we navigate the landscape of AI-driven wealth creation, it is imperative to address ethical considerations to ensure that this transformative technology aligns with sustainability, equity, and social responsibility principles.

The traditional notion of wealth has been closely tied to financial prosperity. However, in the era of AI, wealth extends beyond monetary measures to encompass environmental, social, and ethical dimensions. Achieving a sustainable future requires redefining wealth as a holistic concept that considers economic growth and the well-being of individuals, communities, and the planet.

AI can positively impact wealth creation by enhancing productivity, optimizing resource allocation, and fostering innovation. Automated processes can lead to increased efficiency, reduced waste, and improved decision-making, contributing to economic growth in a sustainable manner. Moreover, AI can be pivotal in addressing global challenges such as climate change, resource depletion, and public health crises.

While the benefits of AI-driven wealth creation are evident, ethical considerations must be at the forefront of its deployment. Unchecked AI development could exacerbate existing societal inequalities, concentrating wealth and power in the hands of a few. It is essential to establish ethical frameworks that guide the development, deployment, and use of AI technologies to ensure they align with fairness, transparency, and inclusivity principles.

One critical aspect of ethical AI wealth creation is the fair distribution of its benefits. Policymakers, businesses, and technology developers must collaborate to design mechanisms that prevent the concentration of wealth and ensure that AI advancements benefit a broad spectrum of society. This involves addressing issues such as job displacement, access to AI education, and the equitable distribution of economic gains.

Transparency is fundamental to ethical AI. Stakeholders, including AI developers and organizations, must be transparent about AI systems' algorithms and data sources. Additionally, accountability mechanisms should be in place to address biases, errors, and unintended consequences that may arise from AI applications. This ensures that AI's decision-making processes are understandable, explainable, and subject to scrutiny.

To mitigate biases in AI systems, promoting inclusivity and diversity in the development process is crucial. Different perspectives, backgrounds, and experiences can help identify and rectify algorithm biases. Inclusivity also ensures that marginalized communities have equal access to the benefits of AI technologies, preventing the creation of digital divides.

The environmental impact of AI must be noticed. As AI systems become more complex and resource-intensive, there is a need to develop sustainable practices in AI development and deployment. This includes optimizing energy consumption, reducing electronic waste, and considering the environmental footprint of AI infrastructure.

Ethical considerations in AI wealth creation require a collaborative and global approach. Governments, industry leaders, and international organizations must work together to establish and enforce ethical standards for AI. This collaborative governance framework should prioritize the interests of humanity, ensuring that AI serves as a tool for collective progress rather than a source of division.

The ethical landscape of AI is dynamic, requiring continuous reflection and adaptation. As AI technologies evolve, so too must ethical frameworks. Regular assessments, audits, and updates are necessary to ensure AI systems align with changing societal values and ethical standards.

The role of AI in a sustainable future is intertwined with ethical considerations in wealth creation. By prioritizing fairness, transparency, inclusivity, and environmental sustainability, we can harness the transformative power of AI to build a future where wealth creation is not only economically robust but also socially equitable and environmentally responsible. The journey towards a sustainable future with AI is a collective endeavor that demands ethical mindfulness and a commitment to the well-being of current and future generations.

# 9. Challenges and Future Trends

Artificial Intelligence (AI) has made remarkable strides in recent years, revolutionizing industries, enhancing efficiency, and enabling breakthroughs in various fields. However, as AI continues to advance, it is accompanied by challenges that raise essential questions about its future trajectory. This chapter delves into AI's challenges and explores the potential future trends that will shape its evolution.

One of the most significant challenges is the ethical implications of AI. As AI systems become more powerful, questions arise about their impact on privacy, security, and human rights. Issues such as bias in algorithms, job displacement, and the potential misuse of AI for malicious purposes demand careful consideration and ethical guidelines.

AI models, intense learning models, are often perceived as black boxes, making it challenging to understand their decision-making processes. The need for more transparency and explainability raises concerns about accountability and trust. Efforts are underway to develop methods for making AI systems more interpretable and accountable.

AI systems heavily rely on vast amounts of data for training and learning. Ensuring the privacy and security of this data is crucial. Data breaches and unauthorized access to sensitive information can have severe consequences, necessitating the development of robust data protection measures.

AI algorithms can inadvertently perpetuate and amplify existing biases present in the training data. This bias can lead to unfair and discriminatory outcomes, especially in hiring, lending, and criminal justice areas. Addressing prejudice and ensuring fairness in AI models is a complex and ongoing challenge.

The rapid advancement of AI has outpaced the development of comprehensive regulatory frameworks. Establishing clear guidelines and regulations to govern the use of AI, especially in critical areas like healthcare and autonomous vehicles, is essential to prevent misuse and ensure responsible AI deployment.

As the demand for transparency grows, the development of Explainable AI (XAI) is gaining momentum. Future AI systems will likely incorporate features that clearly explain their decisions, fostering trust and accountability.

The healthcare industry stands to benefit significantly from AI applications, including diagnostic tools, personalized medicine, and drug discovery. Integrating AI into healthcare systems could lead to more accurate diagnoses, improved patient outcomes, and increased efficiency in medical research.

AI has the potential to contribute to addressing global challenges such as climate change. AI can be crucial in developing sustainable solutions, from optimizing energy consumption to analyzing environmental data for better decision-making.

Natural Language Processing has seen remarkable progress, enabling AI systems to understand and generate human-like language. Future trends may include even more sophisticated language models, with applications ranging from virtual assistants to content creation.

Integrating AI with edge computing allows processing data closer to the source, reducing latency and enhancing real-time decision-making. This trend is particularly relevant in applications like the Internet of Things (IoT) and autonomous vehicles.

As AI continues to evolve, addressing its challenges is crucial for ensuring responsible and ethical development. Simultaneously, exploring future trends holds the promise of transformative advancements across various domains. Striking a balance between innovation and ethical considerations will be vital in shaping the future of AI in a way that benefits humanity as a whole.

## Overcoming AI Implementation Challenges

Artificial Intelligence (AI) has emerged as a transformative force across industries, promising increased efficiency, innovation, and competitiveness. However, the journey from conceptualizing AI applications to successful implementation is challenging. This chapter will explore the common hurdles organizations face when implementing AI and discuss practical strategies to overcome them.

One of the foremost challenges in AI implementation is data availability and quality. Inadequate or poor-quality data can lead to biased models and inaccurate predictions. Organizations must invest in robust data governance practices to overcome this challenge, ensuring data is clean, relevant, and accessible. Implementing data lakes, data cleaning algorithms, and regular audits can contribute to maintaining data quality.

The demand for skilled AI professionals often exceeds the available talent pool. Organizations can address this challenge by investing in training programs for existing employees, collaborating with academic institutions, and leveraging external experts through partnerships or consultancy. Additionally, user-friendly AI development tools can empower non-experts to contribute to AI projects.

Integrating AI solutions with existing systems can be complex and may disrupt normal business operations. Organizations should conduct thorough compatibility assessments to mitigate this challenge, plan for gradual integration, and prioritize interoperability. API-based solutions and modular architecture can facilitate seamless integration with minimal disruption.

AI systems must adhere to ethical standards and regulatory requirements, which vary across industries and regions. Organizations should establish clear ethical guidelines for AI development and deployment to address this challenge. Regular audits and compliance checks help ensure that AI systems meet legal and ethical standards, fostering trust among users and stakeholders.

The "black-box" nature of some AI models can hinder user trust and acceptance. Overcoming this challenge requires a focus on model interpretability. Organizations should opt for models that explain their decisions and invest in tools that help users understand how the AI arrives at specific conclusions. Transparent models contribute to better user acceptance and regulatory compliance.

As AI applications expand, ensuring scalability becomes crucial. To overcome this challenge, organizations should design AI solutions with scalability in mind from the outset. Cloud-based solutions, containerization, and distributed computing architectures are critical in building scalable AI systems that can handle increasing workloads.

AI systems are susceptible to security threats, from data breaches to adversarial attacks on models. Organizations should prioritize security by implementing encryption, access controls, and regular security audits. Collaboration with cybersecurity experts and staying informed about emerging threats are essential in safeguarding AI systems.

Successful AI implementation requires a strategic and holistic approach that addresses various challenges. Organizations must invest in people, processes, and technologies to overcome data, talent, integration, ethics, interpretability, scalability, and security hurdles. By doing so, they can unlock the full potential of AI, driving innovation, efficiency, and competitive advantage in an increasingly AI-driven world.

## Emerging Trends in AI

In the ever-evolving landscape of technology, Artificial Intelligence (AI) continues to be a driving force, transforming industries and reshaping the way we interact with the world. This chapter explores the latest trends emerging within AI, highlighting their potential impact on various sectors and the broader societal landscape.

As AI systems become more sophisticated, there is a growing need for transparency and accountability. Explainable AI, or XAI, addresses the challenge of making AI systems more understandable and interpretable for humans. This trend seeks to demystify the decision-making processes of AI models, allowing users to comprehend the rationale behind their outputs. This is particularly crucial in applications such as healthcare, finance, and autonomous systems, where trust, accountability, and ethical considerations are paramount.

Edge computing involves processing data locally on devices rather than relying on a centralized cloud infrastructure. Edge AI takes this concept further by directly incorporating artificial intelligence into edge devices. This trend reduces latency, enhances privacy, and enables real-time decision-making. Edge AI is gaining prominence in applications like smart cities, industrial IoT, and autonomous vehicles, where instantaneous and decentralized decision-making is critical.

GANs have revolutionized the field of AI by introducing a new paradigm of training models through adversarial learning. This involves two neural networks—the generator and the discriminator—competing against each other. GANs have found applications in image synthesis, style transfer, and creating realistic deepfake content. As this technology matures, its applications will expand into drug discovery, content creation, and virtual reality.

The healthcare sector is witnessing a transformative impact from AI. From predictive analytics for disease prevention to personalized medicine and drug discovery, AI is revolutionizing how healthcare services are delivered. Machine learning algorithms can analyze vast patient data, leading to more accurate diagnostics and treatment plans. Additionally, AI-powered robotics aid surgeries, making procedures more precise and less invasive.

With the increasing integration of AI in decision-making processes, the need for ethical considerations and bias mitigation has become paramount. Efforts are underway to develop frameworks and guidelines to ensure fairness, transparency, and accountability in AI systems. The focus is on addressing biases in training data, establishing ethical standards, and incorporating diverse perspectives in developing and deploying AI technologies.

NLP has made significant strides, enabling machines to understand, interpret, and generate human-like language. This has led to advancements in chatbots, virtual assistants, and language translation services. OpenAI's GPT models are examples of this progress, showcasing the ability to generate coherent and contextually relevant text. NLP is poised to be pivotal in fostering more natural and intuitive interactions between humans and machines.

As the world grapples with the challenges of climate change, AI is emerging as a powerful tool for environmental sustainability. Machine learning algorithms are being applied to analyze climate data, optimize energy consumption, and develop innovative solutions for mitigating environmental impact. AI also contributes to developing intelligent grids, precision agriculture, and renewable energy technologies.

The landscape of artificial intelligence is dynamic and constantly evolving. These emerging trends represent the forefront of AI innovation, potentially reshaping industries, enhancing human capabilities, and addressing complex societal challenges. As we navigate the future of AI, it is imperative to approach these advancements with a careful balance of excitement and ethical consideration to ensure a positive and inclusive impact on society.

## The Future Landscape of AI Wealth Creation

The transformative power of artificial intelligence (AI) will reshape the global economic landscape. As we navigate the uncharted territories of technological advancements, the creation of wealth through AI will become a defining feature of our economic evolution. This chapter explores the multifaceted dimensions of the future landscape of AI wealth creation, encompassing economic, social, and ethical considerations.

Industries fully embracing AI will experience unprecedented growth, efficiency, and innovation. Sectors such as healthcare, finance, manufacturing, and logistics will be at the forefront of this revolution. AI algorithms will optimize processes, predict market trends, and enable personalized experiences, increasing productivity and profitability. As a result, companies that strategically integrate AI into their operations will outpace their competitors and contribute significantly to the global economy.

While AI creates wealth, it also transforms the nature of work. Routine tasks will be automated, leading to the displacement of specific jobs. However, the AI era will also generate new employment opportunities, particularly in AI development, data science, and AI ethics fields. Reskilling and upskilling programs will become imperative for the workforce to adapt to the evolving job market, ensuring that individuals can contribute meaningfully to the AI-driven economy.

As the wealth created by AI accumulates, societies will grapple with the question of inclusivity. Will the benefits of AI wealth creation be distributed equitably, or will they exacerbate existing social and economic inequalities? Policymakers will play a crucial role in shaping the regulatory framework to ensure that the benefits of AI are shared across diverse demographics. Initiatives like universal basic income and education reforms will be explored to mitigate potential disparities.

The ethical implications of AI wealth creation cannot be overstated. Ensuring that AI technologies are developed and deployed responsibly is paramount. To prevent unintended consequences, transparency, accountability, and fairness must be core principles in AI systems. Ethical AI frameworks and guidelines will be established to guide businesses, researchers, and policymakers in navigating the complex landscape of AI ethics.

Given the global nature of AI, international collaboration will be essential to address challenges and harness opportunities. Countries and organizations will collaborate to establish common standards, share best practices, and address ethical concerns on a global scale. A harmonized approach to AI governance will emerge, fostering a collaborative environment that accelerates innovation while safeguarding against potential risks.

The AI-driven economy will spur a wave of entrepreneurial activity. Startups and innovators will seize the opportunity to create niche solutions, disrupting traditional industries and pushing the boundaries of what is possible. Venture capital and investment in AI startups will skyrocket, creating a dynamic ecosystem that fosters innovation and accelerates the pace of technological progress.

The impact of AI wealth creation on the environment cannot be ignored. As energy-intensive AI models become prevalent, concerns about sustainability will rise. Innovations in green AI, energy-efficient algorithms, and responsible computing practices will be imperative to ensure that the benefits of AI wealth creation do not come at the planet's expense.

The future landscape of AI wealth creation holds immense promise, but it also poses challenges that demand thoughtful and proactive responses. As we navigate this uncharted territory, it is crucial to prioritize human-centric values, ethical considerations, and inclusivity. By shaping a future where AI serves humanity, we can unlock the full potential of AI wealth creation while preserving the well-being of individuals and societies. The journey ahead is complex, but with foresight, collaboration, and responsible stewardship, we can build a future where AI enhances the human experience and contributes to a more prosperous and equitable world.

## 10. AI and Society: A New Era of Prosperity

In the early 21st century, artificial intelligence (AI) emerged as a transformative force, reshaping the landscape of industries, economies, and societies. As the integration of AI advanced, it ushered in a new era of prosperity, fundamentally altering how we work, live, and interact. This chapter explores the profound impact of AI on society, the opportunities it presents, and the challenges it poses, ultimately painting a picture of a future characterized by unprecedented prosperity.

The advent of AI marked a pivotal moment in human history, comparable to the Industrial Revolution. Intelligent machines, powered by advanced algorithms and machine learning, began augmenting human capabilities unimaginably. From healthcare to finance and transportation education, AI has infiltrated every sector, optimizing processes and fostering innovation.

Contrary to fears of widespread job loss, the AI revolution sparked a wave of economic growth. As routine tasks became automated, human workers were liberated to focus on creative, strategic, and emotionally intelligent endeavors. New job categories emerged, emphasizing problem-solving, critical thinking, and adaptability. Governments and businesses collaborated to invest in reskilling programs, ensuring the workforce transitioned smoothly into the AI-driven economy.

AI revolutionized healthcare, leading to more accurate diagnostics, personalized treatments, and efficient drug discovery. Machine learning algorithms process vast amounts of medical data, identifying patterns and predicting diseases with unprecedented precision. Virtual health assistants provided real-time support, improving accessibility to healthcare services. The result was a healthier and more informed global population.

Education underwent a radical transformation as AI tailored learning experiences to individual needs. Intelligent tutoring systems adapted to each student's pace and learning style, fostering a more inclusive and effective educational environment. Virtual and augmented reality technologies enriched the learning process, providing immersive experiences transcending traditional classroom boundaries.

The integration of AI into society also raised ethical concerns. The potential misuse of AI, bias in algorithms, and the implications of autonomous systems demanded careful consideration. Governments, industries, and academia collaborated to establish ethical frameworks and guidelines for the responsible development and deployment of AI technologies, ensuring prosperity was coupled with fairness, transparency, and accountability.

AI played a pivotal role in developing smart cities, where interconnected systems optimized resource allocation, reduced environmental impact, and enhanced the quality of life for residents. From efficient traffic management to waste reduction, AI-driven solutions transformed urban spaces into hubs of sustainability and innovation.

While prosperity abounded, the benefits of AI were not evenly distributed. Efforts were made to bridge socioeconomic gaps, with initiatives focusing on digital literacy, affordable access to technology, and inclusive policies. Governments and private entities collaborated to ensure that the benefits of AI were shared equitably, fostering a society that thrived collectively.

As AI became an integral part of the workforce, a new paradigm of collaboration emerged. Humans and machines worked in tandem, each leveraging their unique strengths. Creativity, emotional intelligence, and ethical decision-making became hallmarks of human contributions, while AI handled repetitive data processing tasks and offered valuable insights. This collaborative synergy became the cornerstone of prosperity in the AI-driven society.

The continuous evolution of AI technologies characterized the new era of prosperity. Research and development efforts pushed the boundaries of what was possible, with breakthroughs in quantum computing, explainable AI, and decentralized systems. This ongoing innovation ensured that society remained at the forefront of progress, adapting to emerging challenges and opportunities.

Amid technological advancement, society prioritized a holistic approach to well-being. Emphasizing mental health, work-life balance, and meaningful connections, the AI-driven era sought to enhance the overall quality of life. Cultural shifts encouraged mindfulness, resilience, and a balance between the virtual and physical worlds, fostering a society that thrived economically and in terms of human flourishing.

Integrating AI into society marked the beginning of a new era of prosperity. By addressing ethical considerations, fostering inclusivity, and prioritizing the well-being of individuals, this AI-driven society showcased the potential for technology to be a force for positive change. As the journey continued, society remained vigilant, adaptive, and committed to the principles that ensured the prosperity of all its members in this exciting new age.

## AI and Job Creation

Artificial Intelligence (AI) has ushered in a new era of technological advancements, transforming industries and reshaping the global workforce. As AI matures, there is a growing discourse about its impact on job creation. Contrary to popular fears that automation will lead to widespread unemployment, there is evidence to suggest that AI can be a catalyst for job creation and economic growth.

Historically, technological advancements, including automation, have led to increased productivity and efficiency. While some routine and repetitive tasks may be automated, the overall effect often creates more complex job categories requiring advanced skills. This phenomenon is known as the "automation paradox."

AI technologies, such as machine learning and natural language processing, are increasingly being integrated into various industries, augmenting human capabilities rather than replacing them. For example, AI assists medical professionals in diagnosis and treatment planning in healthcare, leading to improved patient outcomes. This collaboration between humans and AI enhances job roles and opens up new avenues for employment.

As AI takes over routine tasks, the demand for skills in data science, machine learning, and AI programming is rising. Companies are investing in upskilling their workforce to meet the evolving demands of the digital age. Educational institutions are adapting curricula to ensure graduates have the skills to thrive in an AI-driven economy.

The integration of AI has spawned entirely new industries and markets. From autonomous vehicles to virtual reality, these emerging fields demand diverse skills, from AI specialists to creative designers and ethicists. Entrepreneurs and innovators are finding opportunities to create businesses that leverage the power of AI, leading to job creation in unexpected sectors.

While large corporations often spearhead AI adoption, the technology's benefits are not limited to major players. SMEs increasingly harness AI tools to enhance their operations, streamline processes, and remain competitive. This democratization of AI allows smaller businesses to thrive and expand, contributing to local job markets.

Specific jobs require a level of emotional intelligence, creativity, and empathy that AI currently cannot replicate. Professions in healthcare, education, and the arts, for instance, heavily rely on the human touch. As AI handles routine tasks, humans can focus more on these interpersonal aspects of their work, emphasizing the complementary relationship between AI and human skills.

Governments play a crucial role in shaping the impact of AI on job creation. Forward-thinking policies that encourage innovation invest in education and training, and foster a supportive business environment can help maximize the positive outcomes of AI adoption. Additionally, ethical guidelines and regulations can ensure responsible AI development, promoting trust and minimizing potential negative consequences.

The relationship between AI and job creation is dynamic and multifaceted. While automation may lead to the displacement of specific jobs, the overall impact is likely positive, with AI driving economic growth, creating new opportunities, and reshaping work. Strategic investments in education, training, and thoughtful government policies can help societies navigate this transformative period and ensure that the benefits of AI are shared equitably across the workforce.

As the waves of artificial intelligence (AI) innovation crash onto the shores of the job market, the landscape undergoes a profound transformation. The relationship between AI and job creation is a dynamic and intricate dance, reshaping industries, occupations, and the very nature of work itself. In this chapter, we explore the multifaceted impact of AI on employment, the emergence of new opportunities, and the challenges that individuals and societies face in adapting to this rapidly evolving landscape.

One prevailing narrative surrounding AI centers on the fear of massive job displacement, fueled by the belief that machines will replace human workers across various sectors. However, history teaches us that technological advancements often lead to new jobs and industries. The advent of AI is no exception.

Contrary to popular belief, AI is not solely a destroyer of jobs but also a catalyst for job creation. Automation and AI technologies can take over routine, repetitive tasks, allowing human workers to focus on more complex, creative, and value-driven aspects of their roles. The key lies in understanding how AI can augment human capabilities rather than replace them.

As specific jobs become automated, new professions emerge to manage, develop, and maintain AI systems. Data scientists, machine learning engineers, and AI ethicists are just a few examples of roles that have gained prominence in response to the growing influence of AI. These professionals play a crucial role in designing, implementing, and ensuring the ethical use of AI technologies.

Moreover, AI has spurred the growth of interdisciplinary fields, where individuals with diverse skills collaborate to solve complex problems. For instance, the convergence of AI and healthcare has given rise to roles that blend medical expertise with data science, leading to personalized medicine and predictive diagnostics innovations.

Integrating AI into the workforce underscores the importance of continuous learning and adaptability. To thrive in the age of AI, individuals must embrace a culture of lifelong learning and be proactive in acquiring new skills. Governments, educational institutions, and businesses must collaborate to provide accessible and effective reskilling programs, equipping workers with the necessary tools to stay relevant in a rapidly changing job market.

While the potential for job creation is significant, challenges abound. Ethical considerations, such as bias in AI algorithms and the impact of automation on specific industries, require careful attention. Striking a balance between technological innovation and societal well-being is paramount to ensuring a positive and inclusive future for the workforce.

The evolving job landscape in the age of AI is a story of adaptation, innovation, and resilience. As AI continues to shape industries and redefine work, individuals and societies must navigate the waves of change with a forward-thinking mindset. Embracing the opportunities presented by AI, investing in education and reskilling, and addressing ethical considerations will be vital in building a future where AI and human workers coexist, complementing each other to create a more prosperous and inclusive society.

Artificial intelligence (AI) has emerged as a transformative force, reshaping industries and redefining the nature of work. As AI technologies become integral to businesses across sectors, the demand for a skilled AI workforce is skyrocketing. However, this surge in demand has also brought forth a pressing challenge - the need for upskilling and reskilling to ensure that the current workforce remains relevant and adaptable.

As organizations integrate AI technologies into their operations, the job market is witnessing a paradigm shift. Traditional roles are being augmented, and new, specialized positions are emerging. The demand for diverse skill sets is unprecedented, from AI engineers and data scientists to AI ethicists and automation specialists. In this rapidly changing landscape, the ability to upskill and reskill becomes crucial for individual professionals and the workforce.

Upskilling refers to acquiring new skills or enhancing existing ones to meet the demands of evolving technologies. In AI, upskilling is not limited to technical proficiency alone. While proficiency in machine learning algorithms, programming languages, and data analysis is essential, a holistic approach involves fostering a combination of technical, ethical, and soft skills.

**Machine Learning and Data Analysis:** A foundational understanding of machine learning algorithms and data analysis is imperative. Professionals should familiarize themselves with popular frameworks like TensorFlow and PyTorch.

Programming Languages: Proficiency in languages such as Python and R is fundamental for developing and implementing AI solutions

Cloud Computing: Knowledge of cloud platforms like AWS, Azure, or Google Cloud is essential for scalable AI deployment.

**AI Ethics and Bias Training:** Given the ethical challenges associated with AI, professionals need Training in understanding and mitigating biases, ensuring responsible AI development and deployment.

**Privacy and Security:** With the increased use of AI in handling sensitive data, professionals must be well-versed in privacy and security measures to protect user information.

**Critical Thinking and Problem-Solving:** The ability to critically analyze problems and develop creative solutions is invaluable in AI-related roles.

**Communication:** AI professionals should be adept at conveying complex technical concepts to non-technical stakeholders, fostering collaboration across diverse teams.

Reskilling involves equipping individuals with an entirely new set of skills to transition into different roles or industries. As AI disrupts traditional job structures, reskilling is becoming a lifeline for those seeking to adapt to the changing employment landscape.

**Analyzing Existing Skill Sets:** Individuals should assess their current skills and identify transferable ones that can be adapted to AI-related roles.

Cross-Functional Training:* Reskilling may involve cross-functional Training, allowing individuals to apply their expertise to new AI applications.

**Online Courses and Certifications:** Accessible online courses and certifications allow individuals to learn at their own pace, acquiring the skills needed for AI roles.

**Collaboration with Educational Institutions:** Partnerships between industries and educational institutions can facilitate tailored reskilling programs, ensuring alignment with industry requirements.

Recognizing the importance of upskilling and reskilling, governments and corporations play a pivotal role in driving initiatives to bridge the skills gap.

**Funding and Subsidies:** Governments can offer financial incentives to individuals and organizations investing in AI education and training programs.

**National Skill Development Programs:** Launching comprehensive skill development programs that address the specific needs of the AI workforce.

**In-House Training Programs:** Companies can establish in-house training programs to continuously upskill their workforce, ensuring employees stay abreast of AI advancements.

**Collaboration with Educational Institutions:** Partnerships between corporations and educational institutions can facilitate the development of a curriculum that aligns with industry demands.

Upskilling and reskilling are not merely responses to a changing job market but are proactive strategies for individuals and organizations to thrive in the era of AI. The commitment to continuous learning becomes a cornerstone for success as the workforce transforms. By embracing upskilling and reskilling initiatives, we empower individuals to contribute meaningfully to the AI workforce, fostering innovation and ensuring a sustainable future for the global economy.

The integration of artificial intelligence (AI) has become a driving force behind innovation, transforming industries and reshaping the entrepreneurial landscape. As AI technologies advance, entrepreneurs are finding new ways to leverage these tools to create businesses, streamline operations, and generate employment opportunities. This chapter explores the symbiotic relationship between AI, entrepreneurship, and job creation.

The traditional image of an entrepreneur conjures visions of risk-taking individuals starting small businesses and gradually expanding their operations. Today, AI redefines this narrative by offering entrepreneurs powerful tools to innovate and disrupt established industries. AI technologies such as machine learning, natural language processing, and computer vision enable entrepreneurs to automate routine tasks, analyze vast amounts of data, and gain once-impossible insights.

Entrepreneurs are increasingly adopting business models that center around AI applications. For instance, startups utilize AI for personalized marketing, predictive analytics, and customer relationship management. These innovations enhance operational efficiency and open new avenues for revenue generation.

Take the example of a fictitious startup, "InnoTech Solutions," specializing in AI-driven data analytics. By leveraging machine learning algorithms, InnoTech helps businesses derive meaningful insights from their data, enabling them to make informed decisions. This venture provides a valuable service and requires skilled professionals to develop, implement, and maintain AI systems, thus contributing to job creation.

Contrary to popular belief that AI will lead to massive job displacement, many entrepreneurs are proving that AI can catalyze job creation. While specific routine and repetitive tasks may be automated, the demand for skilled workers who can design, implement, and manage AI systems is rising. Moreover, new job categories emerge as AI applications evolve, creating opportunities for individuals with diverse skill sets.

InnoTech Solutions, for example, employs data scientists and machine learning engineers and requires sales, marketing, and customer support professionals. The company's growth ripple effect on the economy creates indirect job opportunities in supply chain management, logistics, and legal services.

Entrepreneurs play a crucial role in shaping the future job market by investing in education and training programs that equip individuals with the skills required in an AI-driven economy. Initiatives such as coding boot camps, online courses, and industry-academic collaborations help bridge the gap between traditional education and the rapidly evolving demands of the job market.

Governments and policymakers can contribute to this effort by creating supportive frameworks encouraging entrepreneurship and innovation. By fostering an environment that embraces AI technologies, they can stimulate economic growth, attract investments, and create new job opportunities.

AI's role in entrepreneurship goes beyond mere automation; it catalyzes innovation, disruption, and, most importantly, job creation. Entrepreneurs leveraging AI technologies are building businesses and contributing to the evolution of the job market. As we navigate the future, it is crucial to recognize the potential of AI in fostering economic growth, empowering entrepreneurs, and shaping a workforce that is not displaced by technology but instead thrives in collaboration with it. Today's entrepreneurs have the opportunity to redefine the narrative, proving that AI is not a threat to jobs but a powerful tool for creating new, meaningful opportunities in the ever-evolving landscape of entrepreneurship.

The rapid advancement of artificial intelligence (AI) has undoubtedly transformed the employment landscape, triggering concerns about job displacement. However, it's crucial to recognize that AI also presents unprecedented opportunities for job creation. This chapter delves into the complexities of addressing job displacement concerns while exploring strategies to foster new employment opportunities in the evolving AI-driven economy.

As AI technologies continue to automate routine tasks, there is a legitimate concern about specific job roles becoming obsolete. Traditional manufacturing, administrative support, and transportation industries may experience significant shifts, leading to workforce disruptions. Acknowledging these challenges and proactively developing strategies to mitigate their impact is imperative.

One of the most effective ways to address job displacement is through comprehensive retraining and upskilling programs. Governments, educational institutions, and private enterprises must collaborate to create accessible and adaptable learning pathways for workers affected by automation. These initiatives should focus on developing skills that complement AI capabilities, such as critical thinking, problem-solving, and creativity.

The era of AI requires a shift toward a culture of lifelong learning. Encouraging individuals to embrace continuous education throughout their careers is essential for adapting to the evolving job market. Employers should invest in educational benefits and flexible work arrangements that enable employees to pursue further education without disrupting their professional lives.

AI automates tasks and opens up new frontiers for entrepreneurship and innovation. Governments and private entities should foster an environment that encourages the creation of startups and supports small and medium-sized enterprises (SMEs). Initiatives such as incubators, grants, and tax incentives can stimulate the growth of businesses that leverage AI technologies, creating diverse job opportunities.

Responsible AI deployment is crucial to mitigating job displacement concerns. Employers should prioritize ethical considerations, transparency, and accountability in AI implementations. Governments can play a role in regulating AI practices to ensure fair treatment of workers and prevent unjustified job losses. Balancing technological advancement with ethical considerations is paramount for building public trust and acceptance of AI.

Collaboration between educational institutions and businesses is essential to bridge the gap between academic knowledge and industry needs. Industry leaders can provide insights into the skills and expertise required in the job market, influencing educational curricula to align with evolving industry demands. Internship programs, apprenticeships, and industry-academic partnerships can facilitate a smoother student transition into the workforce.

Governments and private investors should strategically invest in emerging industries poised to grow with the integration of AI. This includes AI research and development, green technologies, healthcare, and personalized services. By proactively investing in sectors with high potential for job creation, economies can transition more smoothly through periods of job displacement.

Addressing job displacement concerns in the age of AI requires a comprehensive and collaborative approach. By focusing on retraining initiatives, promoting lifelong learning, supporting entrepreneurship, ensuring responsible AI practices, fostering collaboration between industry and academia, and strategically investing in emerging industries, societies can harness the transformative power of AI while minimizing negative impacts on the workforce. The key lies in proactive adaptation, ethical considerations, and a commitment to creating a future where AI enhances human potential rather than replacing it.

Integrating artificial intelligence (AI) into various industries has undeniably transformed the employment landscape, bringing new opportunities and challenges. As organizations harness the power of AI to streamline processes and enhance efficiency, ethical considerations in AI job creation have become paramount. This chapter explores the multifaceted aspects of ethics relating to the intersection of AI and job creation.

One of the primary ethical concerns in AI job creation revolves around fairness and inclusivity. As AI algorithms play a crucial role in the hiring process, there is a risk of perpetuating biases in historical employment data. Developers must ensure that AI systems are trained on diverse datasets, avoiding discrimination based on gender, ethnicity, or other protected characteristics. A commitment to fairness can help prevent the exacerbation of existing societal inequalities.

Maintaining transparency in AI job creation is essential for building trust among job seekers and stakeholders. Organizations should be open about the criteria and algorithms used in the hiring process, allowing individuals to understand how decisions are made. Furthermore, accountability mechanisms must be in place to address potential errors or biases in AI systems, with clear channels for individuals to appeal decisions made by automated processes.

As AI technology evolves, specific job roles may become automated, displacing the workforce. Ethical considerations in AI job creation necessitate a commitment to reskilling and upskilling initiatives. Employers should actively invest in programs that enable employees to acquire new skills and transition into roles that leverage human capabilities alongside AI technologies. This approach ensures that the workforce remains adaptable to the changing employment landscape.

The widespread adoption of AI has raised concerns about the potential displacement of low-skilled jobs. Ethical considerations dictate that organizations should not prioritize short-term profits over the well-being of workers. Efforts should be made to implement AI technologies responsibly, considering the societal impact and exploring ways to create new opportunities for those at risk of job displacement.

AI job creation relies heavily on collecting and analyzing vast amounts of personal data. Ethical considerations demand a robust commitment to data privacy and security. Organizations must implement stringent measures to protect sensitive information and ensure AI algorithms comply with data protection regulations. Job seekers have the right to know how their data is used and should have the option to opt out of certain data collection practices.

A collaborative approach involving various stakeholders, including government bodies, industry leaders, and advocacy groups, is crucial to addressing ethical concerns in AI job creation. Open dialogues and partnerships help establish industry standards, guidelines, and regulations that prioritize the well-being of workers and ensure the responsible development and deployment of AI technologies.

Ethical considerations in AI job creation are integral to shaping a future where technology enhances human potential without compromising fundamental values. As organizations continue to harness the power of AI, a commitment to fairness, transparency, accountability, reskilling, and collaboration is essential to creating a workforce that thrives in harmony with artificial intelligence.

## Impact of AI on Education and Skills

Integrating artificial intelligence (AI) into education has ushered in a new era, fundamentally transforming the landscape of learning and skill development. This chapter explores the multifaceted impact of AI on education and the evolving nature of skills required in a world increasingly shaped by intelligent technologies.

AI in education has enabled the emergence of personalized learning experiences. Adaptive learning platforms leverage machine learning algorithms to tailor educational content to each student's individual needs, pace, and learning styles. This fosters a more inclusive and effective learning environment, catering to diverse abilities and preferences.

Virtual assistants and chatbots, driven by AI, have become integral components of the educational journey. These tools assist students with queries, provide instant feedback, and even offer guidance on study strategies. The presence of AI-driven educational assistants alleviates the burden on educators, allowing them to focus on more personalized and impactful interactions with students.

AI technologies have played a crucial role in breaking down barriers to education. Through speech-to-text and text-to-speech capabilities, AI helps students with diverse learning needs, including those with disabilities, to access educational content more easily. This fosters a more inclusive learning environment, ensuring that education is accessible to all.

Incorporating AI into educational curricula is reshaping traditional subjects and introducing new ones. Students are exposed to AI concepts and applications, preparing them for a workforce where AI literacy is increasingly important. Educational institutions are challenged to adapt their curricula to ensure graduates possess the skills required to navigate a technology-driven world.

As the demand for technical skills continues to rise, AI has become a powerful tool for skill development. AI-driven simulations and virtual reality environments provide hands-on experiences in healthcare, engineering, and finance. This enhances technical skills and cultivates critical thinking, problem-solving, and adaptability.

The integration of AI in education brings forth a set of challenges and ethical considerations. Issues related to data privacy, algorithmic bias, and the potential exacerbation of existing educational inequalities require careful attention. Educators and policymakers must collaborate to establish ethical guidelines and regulations that ensure the responsible deployment of AI in education.

Adopting AI in education necessitates a paradigm shift in the role of educators. Professional development programs must equip teachers with the skills to effectively leverage AI tools, interpret data insights, and create engaging AI-enhanced learning experiences. Continuous learning and adaptability become essential for educators to stay abreast of technological advancements.

Looking ahead, the synergy between AI and education is poised to strengthen. Lifelong learning initiatives supported by AI will become crucial for individuals to remain competitive in a rapidly evolving job market. The challenge lies in ensuring that education systems are agile enough to keep pace with technological advancements and provide continuous learning opportunities.

The impact of AI on education and skills is profound, reshaping how we learn, teach, and prepare for the future. As we navigate this transformative journey, it is imperative to balance embracing AI's potential benefits and addressing the associated challenges. Through thoughtful integration and ethical considerations, AI can be a powerful catalyst for creating a more accessible, inclusive, and technologically literate global education system.

## Fostering Inclusive AI Wealth

The ethical implications and societal impacts of AI-driven wealth creation have become increasingly apparent. As the world witnesses the transformative power of AI, it is crucial to ensure that this technological advancement fosters inclusivity and equitable distribution of wealth. This chapter will explore the challenges and opportunities associated with boosting inclusive AI wealth and outline key strategies for achieving a more equitable future.

The rise of AI has led to unprecedented economic growth and innovation. However, this growth has not been uniform, leading to concerns about exacerbating existing inequalities. Access to AI technologies, education, and opportunities is not evenly distributed, creating a digital divide that mirrors and amplifies socio-economic disparities.

It is essential to recognize and address these disparities at their roots to foster inclusive AI wealth. This involves bridging the gap in access to education, resources, and opportunities, particularly in underserved communities.

One of the first steps toward inclusivity is democratizing access to AI education. Initiatives that provide affordable and accessible AI education for individuals from diverse backgrounds can empower a broader spectrum of society to participate in the AI-driven economy.

Government agencies, private enterprises, and educational institutions should collaborate to create programs that offer scholarships, mentorship, and training opportunities for underrepresented groups. By investing in a diverse talent pipeline, we can ensure that the benefits of AI are shared more equitably.

Creating inclusive AI wealth requires a commitment to ethical AI development. This involves addressing algorithm bias, ensuring fairness in decision-making processes, and promoting transparency in AI systems. Developers must actively engage in ethical considerations throughout the entire AI lifecycle, from data collection and model training to deployment and ongoing monitoring.

Moreover, involving diverse voices in the design and decision-making processes is crucial to preventing the unintentional perpetuation of biases. By fostering a culture of inclusivity within AI development teams, we can build technologies that better serve the needs of a diverse and global society.

There needs to be a shift in the investment landscape to drive inclusive AI wealth. Governments, philanthropists, and impact investors should actively support projects that prioritize social impact alongside financial returns. By directing funds toward AI initiatives that address pressing societal challenges, we can harness the power of technology to create positive and lasting change.

Additionally, fostering collaborations between the public and private sectors can facilitate the development of AI solutions that have a meaningful impact on marginalized communities. These partnerships can help bridge the gap between innovation and real-world application, ensuring that AI technologies contribute to solving pressing social issues.

Governments play a crucial role in shaping the AI landscape through policy development. Establishing robust frameworks that promote inclusivity, accountability, and transparency in AI deployment is essential. This includes regulations that prevent discriminatory practices, promote data privacy, and ensure that the benefits of AI are distributed equitably.

Policy initiatives should also focus on incentivizing businesses to adopt inclusive AI practices. This could involve tax incentives, grants, or other measures that encourage companies to prioritize diversity in their workforce, eliminate biases in AI systems, and contribute to community development.

Fostering inclusive AI wealth is not only a moral imperative but also essential for the long-term sustainability of the AI ecosystem. By democratizing access to education, promoting ethical AI development, encouraging social impact investing, and implementing supportive policy frameworks, we can shape a future where all share the benefits of AI. As we navigate the complex intersection of technology and society, our collective responsibility is to ensure that AI becomes a force for positive change, contributing to a more inclusive and prosperous world.

## 11. Conclusion

In the fast-paced realm of technological innovation, where groundbreaking advancements continually redefine the landscape of possibilities, a beacon of hope emerges for those seeking to revolutionize their financial destinies. The journey through the pages of "The AI Millionaire Maker" has been nothing short of a transformative expedition into the heart of wealth creation, guided by the unparalleled power of Artificial Intelligence (AI). As we embark on the final chapter, we find ourselves standing at the threshold of a conclusion that is not merely the end of a book but the commencement of a new era in financial prosperity.

The preceding chapters have intricately woven a tapestry of knowledge, exploring the symbiotic relationship between humanity and AI, unraveling the mysteries of data-driven decision-making, and delving into the vast potential of machine learning algorithms. From demystifying the complexities of AI to elucidating its role in shaping industries, we have uncovered the blueprint for transforming aspirations into reality.

"The AI Millionaire Maker" has not been a mere theoretical exploration; it has served as a practical guide, bridging the gap between dreams and reality. Through real-world case studies, success stories, and actionable strategies, readers have been equipped with the tools to harness the transformative power of AI in their pursuit of financial abundance.

As we approach the conclusion, we must gaze into the future landscape that awaits those who embrace the principles articulated within these pages. Integrating AI into wealth creation is not a fleeting trend but a seismic shift that will continue to shape the economic panorama for decades. The final chapter invites readers to envision and prepare for the dynamic future.

The conclusion of "The AI Millionaire Maker" is not a termination but an initiation into a mindset—an AI Millionaire Mindset. It is an invitation to cultivate the habits, attitudes, and strategies to propel individuals toward financial prosperity in an AI-driven world. The journey does not end with the last page but extends into the realm of possibilities that await those who dare to dream and act boldly.

As we bid farewell to the chapters that have unfolded, it becomes evident that the intersection of technology and humanity is not a collision but a fusion. This union has the potential to uplift societies, empower individuals, and create a future where financial success is not a privilege but a possibility for all.

In the pages that follow, the conclusion of "The AI Millionaire Maker" awaits, beckoning readers to embrace the wisdom gained, integrate the knowledge acquired, and embark on a journey where the limitless potential of Artificial Intelligence converges with the indomitable spirit of human ambition. The conclusion is not an end; it is a commencement—a proclamation that wealth, empowered by AI, is within reach for those with the courage to seize it.

### The Power of AI to Create Millionaires

One phenomenon stands out as a beacon of boundless potential: Artificial Intelligence (AI). The transformative power of AI has not only revolutionized industries but has also emerged as a formidable force in the creation of millionaires. This chapter delves into the captivating journey of individuals who have harnessed the prowess of AI, becoming the architects of their success and paving the way for a new era of prosperity.

In the early pages of this book, we explored the historical context of AI, its evolution, and its integration into various sectors. Now, let us focus on the entrepreneurs who recognized the seismic shift AI brought to the business landscape. These visionaries seized the opportunity to harness AI's capabilities, transforming their ventures into lucrative enterprises.

Meet Sarah Chang, a trailblazing entrepreneur whose startup utilized AI algorithms to revolutionize personalized healthcare. By leveraging machine learning, her company analyzed vast datasets to predict and prevent diseases, leading to groundbreaking advancements in proactive healthcare. Sarah's journey exemplifies the transformative power of AI, turning her entrepreneurial dreams into a multi-million-dollar reality.

The financial sector has witnessed a profound transformation with the integration of AI. From algorithmic trading to personalized investment strategies, AI has become the secret weapon of financial wizards. John Rodriguez, a once-struggling stock trader, became a millionaire by embracing AI-driven analytics to navigate the complex world of financial markets. His success story underscores AI's limitless possibilities for those with the foresight to integrate it into their financial endeavors.

E-commerce moguls are redefining the online business landscape through the strategic implementation of AI. Emma Turner, a young entrepreneur with an innovative spirit, utilized AI algorithms to enhance customer experience on her e-commerce platform. By understanding user behavior, predicting preferences, and optimizing supply chains, Emma's venture catapulted her into the league of AI millionaires, demonstrating that even in the competitive world of online retail, AI can be the differentiator.

The democratization of AI has opened doors for aspiring entrepreneurs and visionaries from diverse backgrounds. Startups and individuals with limited resources can now harness the power of cloud-based AI services, leveling the playing field. The story of Raj Patel, a self-taught coder from a small town, showcases how accessible AI tools and platforms enabled him to create a groundbreaking application, ultimately leading to his millionaire status.

As we conclude this chapter, the resounding theme is clear – AI has emerged as the great equalizer in the world of wealth creation. The narratives of Sarah, John, Emma, and Raj highlight that the AI millionaire maker is not an exclusive club; instead, it is an inclusive realm where innovation, determination, and a strategic embrace of AI can pave the way to financial abundance.

The journey toward becoming an AI millionaire is not without its challenges, but the stories within this chapter illustrate that the rewards far outweigh the risks. The AI Millionaire Maker is not a mythical concept; it is a tangible reality for those willing to explore, experiment, and embrace the transformative power of AI. As we navigate the uncharted territories of the future, let this chapter inspire aspiring entrepreneurs, urging them to unleash wealth with artificial intelligence and join the ranks of the AI millionaires who have redefined success in the 21st century.

### Your Journey to AI Wealth Begins Now!

As you embark on this transformative journey into artificial intelligence, you are setting foot on a path that can reshape not only your financial future but also the fabric of how wealth is created and sustained in the digital age. Welcome to "The AI Millionaire Maker: Unleashing Wealth with Artificial Intelligence." In this groundbreaking book, we will delve into the intricacies of AI, unraveling its mysteries and unveiling the unprecedented opportunities it presents for those willing to seize them.

To embark on this journey, you must first adopt the AI mindset. This is not merely about understanding algorithms or programming languages; it's about embracing a new way of thinking. The AI mindset transcends conventional boundaries, pushing you to question the status quo and explore uncharted territories. It demands a curiosity for innovation and a hunger for knowledge that propels you beyond the limits of traditional wealth-building strategies.

Artificial intelligence is not just a technological advancement; it's a catalyst for wealth creation on an unprecedented scale. The convergence of data, algorithms, and computing power has given rise to a landscape where opportunities abound for those who can navigate it skillfully. Whether you are an aspiring entrepreneur, a seasoned investor, or someone seeking to enhance your professional skill set, AI offers the potential to unlock previously unimaginable wealth.

As we journey through the chapters of this book, we will navigate the diverse landscape of AI applications that span industries such as finance, healthcare, education, and beyond. You will discover how AI revolutionizes business processes, optimizes decision-making, and creates entirely new business models. Each chapter will unfold a new layer of the AI universe, providing you with insights, case studies, and practical strategies to capitalize on the wealth-generating potential of AI.

Your journey to AI wealth requires more than theoretical knowledge; it demands a hands-on approach. Throughout this book, we will guide you in building your AI toolkit. From understanding the basics of machine learning to exploring advanced neural networks, you will gain the skills to navigate the complexities of AI implementation. Practical exercises and real-world examples will empower you to apply AI concepts to your unique circumstances.

"The AI Millionaire Maker" is not just about accumulating wealth; it's about unleashing your full potential. As you absorb the knowledge within these pages, consider how AI can amplify your capabilities and impact. This is a journey of self-discovery as much as it is a journey of financial empowerment.

Your journey to AI wealth begins now; the future is yours to shape. The opportunities presented by artificial intelligence are vast, but success will favor those who are proactive, adaptable, and committed to continuous learning. As you conclude this introductory chapter, embrace the possibilities that lie ahead and commit to seizing the future that AI has in store for those bold enough to pursue it.

In the following chapters, we will delve into the specifics of AI applications, investment strategies, and the ethical considerations of wielding such transformative power. Let "The AI Millionaire Maker" be your guide as you embark on a journey that has the potential to redefine not just your financial status but your entire way of life. The future is AI, and the time to shape it is now.

## Appendix: Resources for Further Learning

1. TensorFlow
   [https://www.tensorflow.org/](https://www.tensorflow.org/)
   - An open-source machine learning framework developed by Google. TensorFlow provides tools, libraries, and community resources for building AI models.

2. PyTorch [https://pytorch.org/](https://pytorch.org/)
   - A popular deep learning framework that is widely used for building and training neural network models. PyTorch has a strong community and extensive documentation.

3. Towards Data Science [https://towardsdatascience.com/](https://towardsdatascience.com/)
   - A Medium publication that covers a wide range of topics related to data science, machine learning, and AI. It features insightful articles and tutorials.

4. AI Weekly [https://aiweekly.co/](https://aiweekly.co/)
   - A curated newsletter that delivers a weekly roundup of the latest news, research, and developments in artificial intelligence.

5. OpenAI Blog [https://www.openai.com/blog/](https://www.openai.com/blog/)
   - Explore the blog of OpenAI, the organization behind the development of GPT-3. It provides in-depth insights into AI research and applications.

6. MIT Technology Review - Artificial Intelligence [https://www.technologyreview.com/topic/artificial-intelligence/](https://www.technologyreview.com/topic/artificial-intelligence/)
   - Stay informed about the latest AI advancements, research, and ethical considerations through MIT's renowned Technology Review.

7. AI Ethics [https://aiethics.stanford.edu/](https://aiethics.stanford.edu/)
   - Stanford University's Center for Ethics in Society provides resources on the ethical implications of AI, offering valuable insights into responsible AI development.

8. AI for Everyone - Andrew Ng on YouTube
[https://www.youtube.com/playlist?list=PLQosVbIj3URf96k5CJij
s6LQzoFdAC8jU](https://www.youtube.com/playlist?list=PLQos
VbIj3URf96k5CJijs6LQzoFdAC8jU)
 Access a series of video lectures by Andrew Ng on the
fundamentals of AI. Perfect for both beginners and those looking
to deepen their understanding.

9. Analytics Vidhya
[https://www.analyticsvidhya.com/](https://www.analyticsvidhya
.com/)
 - A platform that offers a plethora of resources, including articles,
tutorials, and forums, to support learning in data science and
machine learning.

10. AI World  [https://aiworld.com/](https://aiworld.com/)
 - Attend virtual or in-person conferences, webinars, and events
through AI World to stay connected with the AI community and
industry trends.

These websites cover a wide range of topics, from practical coding
and implementation to theoretical discussions on the future of AI.
Regularly exploring these resources will keep you informed and
engaged in the dynamic field of artificial intelligence.